WITHIN FOUR WALLS

A CLASSIC *of* ESCAPE

MAJOR M.C.C. HARRISON DSO MC
CAPTAIN H.A. CARTWRIGHT MC

Pen & Sword
MILITARY

First published in Great Britain in 1930 by Edward Arnold & Co.

Reprinted in this format in 2016 by
Pen & Sword Military
An imprint of
Pen & Sword Books Ltd
47 Church Street, Barnsley
South Yorkshire
S70 2AS

ISBN 978 1 47382 757 8

A CIP catalogue record for this book is
available from the British Library

Printed and bound in England
By CPI Group (UK) Ltd, Croydon, CR0 4YY

Pen & Sword Books Ltd incorporates the Imprints of Pen & Sword Aviation,
Pen & Sword Family History, Pen & Sword Maritime, Pen & Sword Military,
Pen & Sword Discovery, Pen & Sword Politics, Pen & Sword Atlas,
Pen & Sword Archaeology, Wharncliffe Local History, Leo Cooper,
Wharncliffe True Crime, Wharncliffe Transport, Pen & Sword Select,
Pen & Sword Military Classics, The Praetorian Press, Claymore Press,
Remember When, Seaforth Publishing and Frontline Publishing

For a complete list of Pen & Sword titles please contact
PEN & SWORD BOOKS LIMITED
47 Church Street, Barnsley, South Yorkshire, S70 2AS, England
E-mail: enquiries@pen-and-sword.co.uk
Website: www.pen-and-sword.co.uk

INTRODUCTION

This book was originally published in 1930. It thus has the benefit of coming into print some years after the war's end and after the fevered demand for 'Boy's Own' type reads that characterized the immediate post-war years had died down. Indeed, an explanation is offered for the frequent use of 'Hun' ('to which the German has always strongly objected') – this was, the authors say, because Cartwright's part of the book is based on an unpublished manuscript that he wrote for his family on his return to Britain.

The account is that of the attempted and ultimately successful escapes of two officers. M.C. Harrison was an officer in the Royal Irish Regiment (on its disbandment upon the creation of the Irish Free State he transferred to the Royal Tank Corps). He was a member of the 2nd Battalion (8 Brigade, 3rd Division), which suffered heavy casualties at Mons and Le Cateau in the early days of the war. By the time of his wounding and capture at Le Pilly (Aubers Ridge) on 19 October 1914, he was the last officer in the battalion who had not become a casualty. His contribution to the book is based on the report he wrote as part of the debriefing following his successful escape in September 1917.

H.A. Cartwright served with the 4th Battalion Middlesex Regiment (also in 8 Brigade, 3rd Division) and was captured in the first BEF action of the war at Mons; he made his escape in the early days of August 1918 and, when finally permitted to return to the Front, got as far as Boulogne only to be greeted with the news of the signing of the Armistice.

Both of the authors state in the introduction that these accounts, written immediately after they made it back to Britain, ensure that the factual elements are therefore not reliant on distant memory. However, they filled in the details that were considered relatively unimportant or unnecessary at the time (or, in Cartwright's case, could not be included because the war was still being fought at the time of writing, which he did for family and friends). The book was the outcome of an evening in 1929 that the two spent together at the home of a friend, recollecting their time as prisoners of the kaiser.

This book must have been required reading for the German authorities (not to mention would-be 'escapers – or 'maniacs' as they were sometimes known by less enthusiastic prisoners) who where responsible for the running of Prisoner of War camps in the Second World War; if it was not, it certainly should have been. The methods and the means used by the two to make their escapes test credulity. They seem to have been able to make full use of their bank accounts in the UK – thus, for example, they were able on one occasion to pay for taxis for themselves and their guards when they were recaptured, not to mention meals (and, in one memorable case, a new bath) and even the cost of legal defence at a German court martial. They developed a complex system of communications, involving codes and invisible ink. They were able to order clothes from their tailors – in one case including a fictional uniform that would be more easily converted to a civilian look. The escape of Major Charles Fox, Scots Guards – captured near Gheluvelt in October 1914 – in June 1917 was a major boost, as he was able to brief families of PoWs far more satisfactorily about what they should be sending and how.

There are detailed descriptions of how 'mobilization' (i.e. in this case escape) stores were hidden away in packages sent from home – cunning use of tins and soap, for example, and even a message secreted in the kernel of a prune. Quite as ingenious were the methods used to retrieve these from the parcels' room in the various camps. The escapers became experts in tailoring (Harrison comments on how he had to make the stitching look as though it were machined and pressing clothes by the use of his thumb nail), lock picking, making keys, finding ever more inspired means of hiding stores (and the Germans failed to find an extraordinary variety of things, despite frequent searches) and German money, bribing guards, identifying spies ('stool pigeon' seems to have been a Second World War expression for such people) and the occasional agent provocateur, making rubber stamps, creating German documentation – and so the list goes on.

As both had several unsuccessful escapes between them they were able to learn from the experience. Strategies had to be adopted – such as when to stop to find effective hiding places during the day, what to carry, what supplies were necessary, how to approach the frontier and so forth – and were all developed and refined. In addition to the lessons learnt from their failures, they had the benefit of those of other officers who had also failed to make it to neutral territory.

Although they suffered at the hands of unfeeling captors, they also make a point of mentioning Germans who were kind or gentlemanly. When Harrison was captured, quite badly wounded, he and fellow British soldiers were quite evidently low on the list of the German medical staff priorities and then had to face a senior doctor who was quite determined to make them as uncomfortable as possible. Yet their actions are contrasted with his experience in a Roman Catholic hospital, run by the St John of God Order, to which he was taken in Dortmund. The head of the community is described as 'one of the finest specimens of the human race that I have ever come across' (amongst other things, he gave Harrison and the other severely wounded British officer with him his own room). Cartwright comments on the commandant at Zorndorf, Reserve Captain Trettner. The camp 'was a hole in the ground and nothing could make it fit for prolonged habitation, but anything which it was possible to do to better the lot of his prisoners he did willingly and generally without being asked'; he delivered a (only marginally out of date) copy of *The Times* to Cartwright, usually personally and normally every day; he attended many of his innumerable courts martial and often spoke in his defence; and even treated him to a meal in a train restaurant car, ignoring the comments of other officers who were affronted that a British PoW should be so treated. It was due to him that Cartwright was sent to Aachen, just prior to his escape.

Although written in a style typical of the time, in what would best be described as British understatement, it is not difficult to get below the surface and realize just how innovative, intelligent, determined, versatile, gifted, persevering and, above all, very brave these two officers were – as, indeed were other escapers, such as Jocelyn Hardy (see *I Escape!*, reprinted by Pen & Sword in 2014). It is possible for a reader to skim over some of their hardships because of the written style: Harrison spent 'over seven months' in 'one of the smallest cells imaginable' in the civilian jail at Magdeburg – it was only 3'4" x 10'6". The description of the tunnel at Torgau (used for an escape in August 1916) is given in a rather off-hand way, but it was an extraordinary feat of construction and engineering, eight months in the construction, which had to go under the fortress walls and then a moat. A good length of it was 21 inches wide and 27 inches high – the whole tunnel being some hundred yards long with fifteen men working on it. In the end nineteen officers, mainly Russian and British, but also a French officer, made their escape, but not before enduring almost three hours entombed in the narrow space before it was determined that the coast was clear.

In addition to sketches and good, clear plans of a number of German PoW camps ('abort' means latrines), there are also some excellent photographs. One of the most moving of these is a group of four officers (including Harrison) after they had made their escape and successfully reached Holland in early September 1917. Included in the group is Gilbert Insall VC and Claude Templer, Glosters, who escaped in company with Harrison and Gerald Knight, Devons and RFC, who escaped at the same time and from the same room but independently (and by an extraordinarily audacious method).

Insall won his VC in late 1915, one of the earliest VCs of the air arm. After his escape he returned to flying duties in both the First and Second World Wars and died in 1972. Claude Templer, 1/Glosters, was wounded and captured in December 1914 at Givenchy. He made thirteen escape attempts. He returned to France in March 1918, shortly after the opening of the German Spring Offensive; the authorities were not keen on returning escaped PoWs to the front at which they were captured and, reluctantly, would only do so at the written and express request of the officer concerned. They were fearful that if they were captured again they might face a very unpleasant second captivity. He was killed by a shell in June 1918 and is commemorated on the Loos (Dud Corner) Memorial. Gentlemen cadets, when roving eyes seek inspiration during Church Parade in the architecturally undistinguished chapel at Sandhurst, will find a prominent memorial tablet that lists his deeds. He was, the memorial notes, a war poet. Knight died shortly after the end of the war, in October 1919.

Harrison went back to his regiment at the Front in December 1917, which then suffered badly in the opening stages of the Ludendorff offensives when it formed part of Fifth Army. It was amalgamated with other battalions but was reformed in April 1918 and he served out the rest of the war with them, this time as commanding officer. He was wounded a few months before the end of the war, which gave him an opportunity to meet up with Cartwright after his own escape, in the dying months of the war, and to act as best man at his wedding (they sent the commandant at Magdeburg a copy of the wedding photograph).

Cartwright remained in the army post war (as did Harrison); possibly his most suitable posting was to Berne, as Military Attaché, where he helped those who had made a home run to Switzerland, amongst whom was Airey Neave.

Finally, my thanks to Jack Sheldon for recommending this book for reprint, who read it when he was a young lad. In preparing this introduction I have read it three times – this was certainly no chore, as it very well written; and it well deserves such close attention.

Nigel Cave,
Worthing 2015

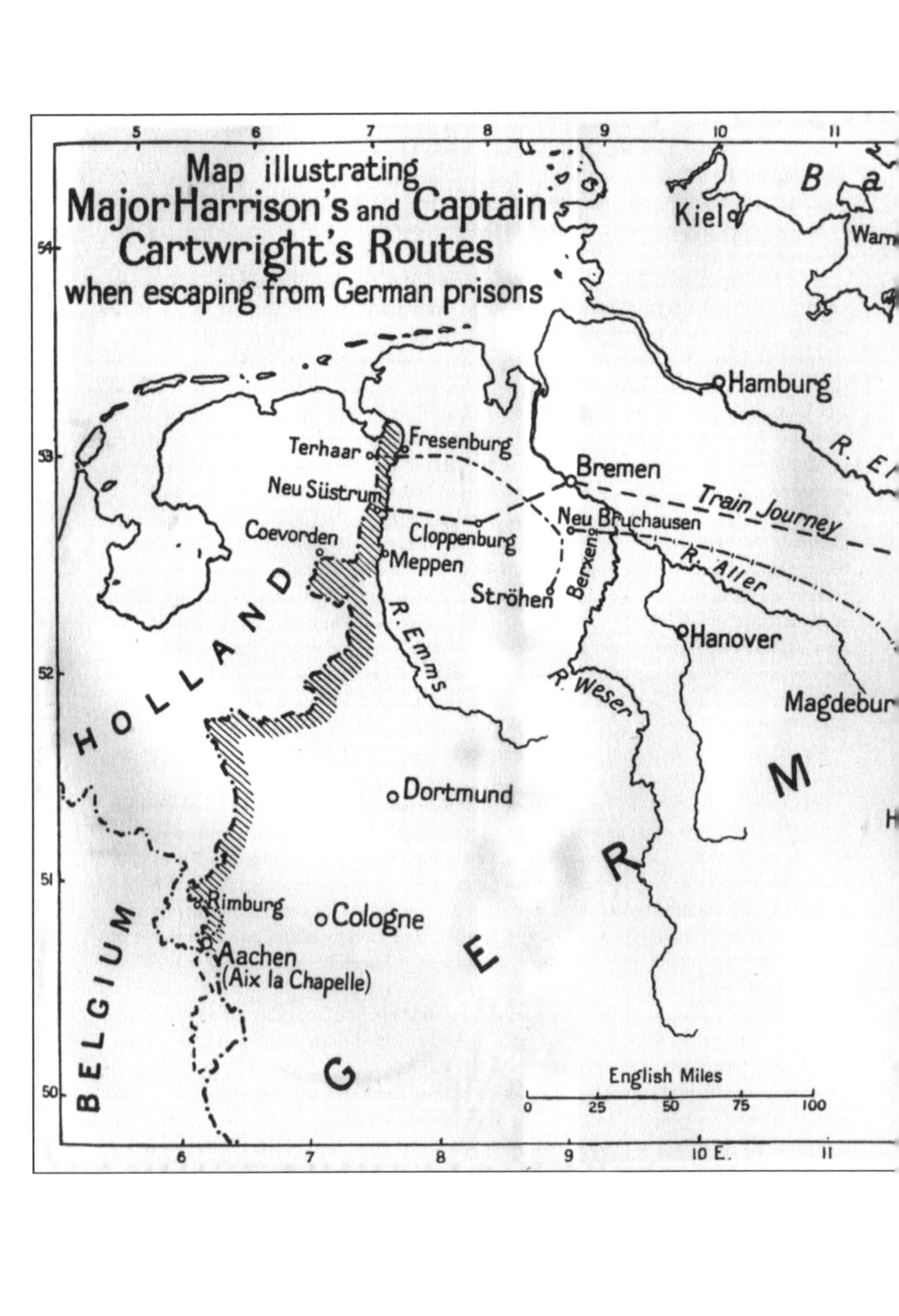
Map illustrating
Major Harrison's and Captain
Cartwright's Routes
when escaping from German prisons
Kiel
Hamburg
R. El
Bremen
Train Journey
Fresenburg
Terhaar
Neu Süstrum
Coevorden
Cloppenburg
Neu Bruchausen
Meppen
Ströhen
Berxen
R. Aller
Hanover
R. Emms
R. Weser
Magdebur
HOLLAND
Dortmund
Rimburg
Cologne
Aachen
(Aix la Chapelle)
BELGIUM
G E R M
English Miles
0 25 50 75 100
5 6 7 8 9 10 11
54 53 52 51 50
6 7 8 9 10 E. 11

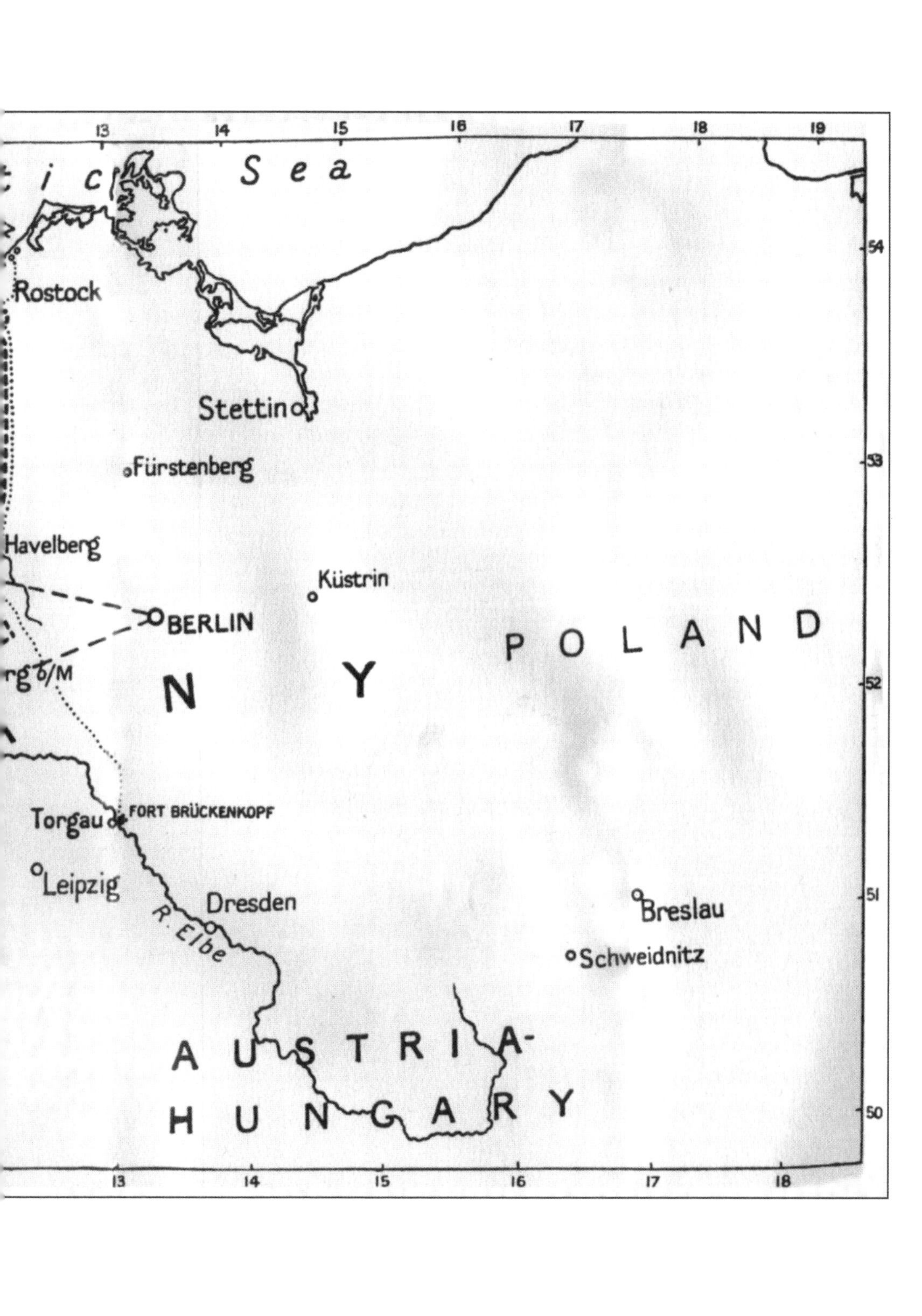

13
14
15
16
17
18
19
i c
Sea
54
Rostock
Stettin
53
Fürstenberg
Havelberg
Küstrin
BERLIN
POLAND
rg a/M
N
Y
52
Torgau
FORT BRÜCKENKOPF
Leipzig
Dresden
R. Elbe
51
Breslau
Schweidnitz
AUSTRIA-
HUNGARY
50
13
14
15
16
17
18

PREFACE

PRESSURE to write the story of our joint and separate experiences in Germany was brought to bear on each of us from many sides as soon as we reached home—one in 1917, the other in 1918—but, with the war still in full swing, we both left it at that.

An official account, short and concise, but quite complete, of the principal events narrated in Chapters I, III, V, and VI of this book was, however, required by the War Office, and it was with this, his own official account, before him, that the author of those chapters wrote them as they now appear.

Chapters II, IV, and VII were, as far as concerns the narrative, written in 1918 for the information of their writer's family, immediately after his return from Germany. Notes on various subjects, which were mentioned incidentally in the original account, but which were not essential to it or could not be discussed while the war was still in progress, were added in 1928–9 and have now been incorporated in the story. It is because so much of these last chapters is reproduced word for word as it was written in 1918 that frequent use is made of the word "Hun" to which the German has always strongly objected.

Even though the narrative was not put together until this year the authors have not had to fall back, therefore, upon memory, but have each had the full facts before them as they were written down at the first possible opportunity.

When we met for the first time in England, in September 1918, for the ceremony at which one of us figured as bridegroom and the other as best man, we decided definitely that if ever we did come to write the story of our experiences it should take the form of a joint account.

A few days after the Armistice we met at Mons and actually got as far as roughing out some headings for a book before we were sent to opposite ends of Europe.

Not coming in touch again for eleven years, we neither of us gave the matter a serious thought until last summer, when a meeting was arranged for us at the house of a mutual friend within half a dozen miles of the barracks in which we had both mobilized. The perpetrator of the illustrations in the text brought to the meeting the originals of most of them, together with his somewhat battered account, and we spent the evening living again through the whole of those long, worst years of our lives.

That evening's talk, coupled with the still increasing pressure of the many relations and friends who failed to give us due credit for the distinction of being among the few prison-breakers who had ever resisted the temptation to appear in print, has resulted finally in the publication of this book.

Official permission to publish has of course been obtained, but the authors are directed to state that they are responsible for the book and that the War Office accepts no responsibility for any statement in it.

THE AUTHORS

July 1930

CONTENTS

PAGE

I. Mons to Burg (*M. C. C. Harrison*) . . 1

In France, August 1914—Taken prisoner—In hospital at Dortmund—Fort Brückenkopf, Torgau—Preparations for escape—Removal to Burg.

II. Burg (*H. A. Cartwright*) 23

Captured at Mons—Journey to Germany—Torgau—At Burg—Plans for escape—In the civil jail—Camp spies—Clothes for escape—Planning a route—Tailoring and dyeing operations—A fiasco—Walking out of Burg camp with Harrison—Nine days of freedom—Recapture at Rostock—Journey back to Burg—The Germans as searchers—Removal to Halle and Torgau.

III. Torgau (*M. C. C. Harrison*) 79

Collecting of stores—Secret information in parcels—Methods of escape—Walks on parole—Campbell's tunnel—Mobilisation kit—Escape with Lesaffres through the tunnel — Walking to the Baltic — Recapture on the coast—Return via Berlin to Torgau—Planning escape from Torgau civil prison—A court martial—Removal to Magdeburg.

IV. Halle and Magdeburg (*H. A. Cartwright*) . 117

Camp at Halle—Removal to Fürstenberg—Back to Burg—Hiding-places for contraband—Removal to Magdeburg—Sawing bars and forging passes—Walking out of camp with Marshall—Doing the sights of Berlin—By train across Germany—Crossing the Emms—Recapture on the frontier at Neu Süstrum—Return to Magdeburg—How stores were received from home—The parcels room—'Escape' parcels.

PAGE

V. MAGDEBURG PRISON (*M. C. C. Harrison*) . 165

In the civil prison at Magdeburg—Possibilities for escape—Obtaining a skeleton key—The parcels office—Cartwright's arrival—A ruined opportunity of escape—Clothes for a daylight escape—A 'spy-hole' picture—Dyeing a coat—Moving cells—Escape with Cartwright from the prison—A two hundred miles' walk—Recapture—Return to Magdeburg—My courts martial—Collecting contraband stores—A last effort with the key.

VI. STRÖHEN (*M. C. C. Harrison*) . . . 221

Description of camp—Plans for escape—The bathroom trap-door—Preparations for walk to Holland—A nine days' walk—Crossing the frontier. A quarantine camp—ENGLAND.

VII. KÜSTRIN, SCHWEIDNITZ AND AACHEN . . 253
(*H. A. Cartwright*)

Fort Zorndorf—The communication tunnels—Courts martial in Berlin—Tricks that failed—German military justice—A successful appeal—A good Prussian—The Russians at Zorndorf—Move to Schweidnitz—Plans for escape—Transfer to Aachen—Escaping from Aachen—An out-of-date map—The frontier at last—Rotterdam—The War Office—The Armistice.

VIII. CONCLUSION (*M. C. C. Harrison*) . 305

LIST OF ILLUSTRATIONS

Map of the Author's Routes vi

Bourcier's escape 15

Plan of Burg 36

The Escape Ceremonial 53

A stroll through Rostock 68

Plan of Torgau 84

I did not notice the commandant 86

The double-backed packing-case 122

"All correct!" 134

This is what we felt like 138

The real and the false keys 172

A general peeps through the spy-hole 185

Magdeburg Prison 192

Officers and gentlemen 200

"Special Constabulary" at Neu Bruchausen 205

The Landsturm were not very bright but – 206

The Military Police 207

A court martial 213

Plan of Ströhen 226

A wasted penny 263

Passing the post 298

WITHIN FOUR WALLS

I

MONS TO BURG

By M. C. C. HARRISON

In France, August 1914—Taken prisoner—In hospital at Dortmund—Fort Brückenkopf, Torgau—Preparations for escape—Removal to Burg.

PROBABLY most of us have vivid recollections of nightmares at some time or other in our lives. On these occasions, perhaps when on the very verge of death, we have woken up to the pleasant reality of finding ourselves in a comfortable bed and merely the victims of an unpleasant dream. I have yet to meet the person who does not remember the tremendous relief experienced when first waking up.

How many of us can reverse the situation? If my readers will admit the probability of dreaming about that which is uppermost in one's mind at the time of going to sleep, they may, before proceeding much further, be able to form some idea of the excessive number of pleasant dreams I must have had as a prisoner, only to wake up on each occasion to a horrible reality.

To be struggling desperately for something for days, weeks, months and even years, will, as time goes on, cause the brain to give little thought to anything else. Unless of a pessimistic nature, what is more natural than to dream that your efforts have met with success and that your great ambition has at last been achieved?

Imagine the pleasure of those dreams, particularly when during them you apparently take the precaution of assuring yourself that 'anyhow it's not a dream this time.' But think of the feeling on waking up. First to see a wall, then another—by now you are fully awake and you see four walls, sometimes almost touching you. You then realise that fate has decreed that you are not to be allowed to focus your eyes on anything beyond those four walls. If you are lucky perhaps you may be allowed outside them, for a brief period, but only into a space where you are again surrounded by four walls.

Oh, what a ghastly sight can four walls be, when viewed perpetually from within!

Most of us can in all probability appreciate the feelings of the rider of No. 13 in the Grand National when the drink died out of him as he approached Becher's Brook in company with a loose horse. That the sight of 'Four Walls' when viewed from within is considered by some to be the worst view in Europe may possibly never have occurred to many.

It is easy to be wise after an event, but with the information available at the time a plan is frequently adopted which, as events develop, may appear to the arm-chair critic as ridiculous. This is the only explanation I can offer for not adopting a more obvious and wiser course on many of the occasions that I am about to narrate. The unprecedented and peculiar conditions caused information, even on trivial matters, to be both rare and unreliable.

At the outbreak of hostilities in 1914 there were few, even amongst the experts of all nationalities, who visualised a war of such magnitude. To the majority a speedy termination seemed a certainty.

As a twenty-six-year-old subaltern in the Royal Irish Regiment stationed at Devonport in 1914 I can perhaps be excused for sharing this popular opinion.

I thought myself very fortunate when I landed at Rouen, on the 11th August 1914, with the advance party of the 3rd Division, and felt genuinely sorry for those who might not arrive before the end of the war.

My regiment lost about twenty-five per cent. of their strength at Mons on the 23rd August. Three days later, at Le Cateau, we lost the remainder of the battalion except five officers and about one hundred and twenty men. In our first two actions we had sustained more casualties than during the whole of the South African War.

At the end of the retreat our first reinforcement arrived. By the 19th October 1914 we had received eight lots of reinforcements, some being as strong as three hundred and fifty. Our losses and the strenuous nature of the fighting in those early days absolutely astounded me. I had begun to think that I had a charmed life, as all the original officers, except myself, had become casualties.

On the afternoon of the 19th October, the 2nd Royal Irish Regiment attacked the village of Le Pilly on the Aubers Ridge on the left and slightly in advance of the remainder of the British Army. A French attack at the same time on Fournes, one and a half miles on our left, failed. Our attack was partially successful and left us in possession of half the village, not an enviable position, as we were now more or less isolated.

Early on the following day the Germans attacked heavily. Antwerp having fallen a few days previously they were able to mass great strength, and a desperate fight raged all day. I was wounded in the left arm about 8 a.m. By 10 a.m., when the situation appeared to be easier, I was wounded in the left hip. I was bringing a message to battalion headquarters at the time. Being still able to crawl on my back I got there about 11 a.m., and when the doctor had dressed my wounds I was put in a cellar in a small cottage with some other wounded. At midday there seemed to be every chance of holding off the enemy. I must then have fallen asleep for my next recollection was hearing Germans above. Soon they came into the cellar, and going round the edge removed everybody except me. I was lying in the middle of the floor and had not been noticed. I was greatly relieved, as I felt sure our reserves would counter-attack at any moment.

At the worst I felt I would be able to crawl up the stairs and back to our own lines during the night. Not until our own doctor came back after dark with two Germans to carry me to a room at the railway station did I realise how helpless I was. By now I was too stiff to move at all.

I then learnt the awful tragedy that had befallen the battalion. A thousand strong on the previous day all except about three hundred had been killed and the survivors, mostly wounded, were all prisoners.

For the next three days fighting was still terrible in the neighbourhood and the Germans, with their superior numbers, were able to gain ground.

The plight of our wounded during these days was not an enviable one. We were left lying in the waiting-room at the station. Our own doctor was able to give us a certain amount of attention and get us food by collecting emergency rations from our dead. There was no German doctor available, so ours worked incessantly day and night for three days attending to the wounded of both sides. With such an enormous number of casualties there was really nothing the Germans could have done during this period to improve conditions. Naturally, their own wounded had to receive primary consideration.

The officer commanding the detachment that

had captured us frequently came and spoke to me. He was a pleasant man of about thirty-six years of age and I should imagine an excellent soldier; he was elated with his victory and collected many souvenirs from us in the way of regimental badges, buttons, etc. Curiously enough he was captured several months later by my regiment, which was re-formed. He recognised our regimental badge, and his account of the battle of Le Pilly was taken down and forwarded to the War Office. Three years later I was called upon to write my version, and it is worthy of record that the two accounts agree.

The evacuation of the wounded was completed on 23rd October, and I was the last by several hours to be removed. The under-officer in charge arrived in an intoxicated condition. For quite an hour he stood over me, periodically waving a naked sword to see how close he could hit without actually touching me.

On arrival at Marouilles, a village three miles in the rear, I was brought to a schoolroom where about forty of our wounded were lying on the floor. Finding the stretcher very comfortable after three days on concrete, I asked if I could remain on it for the night. The answer was promptly to turn it upside down for me to fall out on the floor.

Presently all our overcoats were removed for the German wounded. The nights by now were bitterly cold, and most of the prisoners had had their other garments cut away to enable our doctor to dress their wounds. The next morning I felt really bad as a result of the foul atmosphere, and on the arrival of a German doctor, Herr Scherning, I was carried outside and placed on a chair at my own request.

When the head doctor arrived I was the first person he saw. He wanted to know 'what the hell I was doing out there?' And without waiting for any explanation hit me with such force that I was knocked on to the ground. He then had me dragged into an empty room. Presently the other English wounded were brought there and the under-officer in charge started packing them at the opposite end of the room to where I lay. Suddenly noticing me he let forth a roar, seized me by the neck and kicked me across the floor.

When the room was full the head doctor came in with one of our rifles and a quantity of ammunition. He told us we were all going to be shot as he had found dum-dum ammunition on one of the English. To my request that the man be produced for an explanation he replied, 'It was off a dead man.'

He then showed us how our rifles were specially designed to enable every man to make his own dum-dum ammunition. He got this from a diagram in one of the principal German papers, which I myself saw later on. He placed the butt on the floor and forced the nose of a bullet into the hole at the end of the cut-out, and then using all his force managed to break a bit off the nose. It was a difficult operation, and only succeeded with the ammunition manufactured in certain years. He continued doing this for three days, and gave orders that the English were to receive no medical attention. Beyond a cup of soup once a day, we were given nothing to eat or drink. When Herr Scherning was on duty he arranged, contrary to orders, to attend to our worst cases. Finding my arm was broken in two places, he got hold of a young specialist to set it. That I subsequently recovered the use of my left hand is entirely due to the skill of this man. In order to avoid detection by the head doctor he had little time at his disposal. Holding my hand securely he placed a foot against my shoulder, pulled as hard as he could, turned the arm outwards and then carefully attached a splint. Primitive as the method was, there was practically no pain till he released his grip.

On the 26th October we started our long train journey into Germany, bound for Hamburg. The forty English and a guard were put into a cattle truck, while the German wounded occupied the rest of the train. Before leaving Marouilles the head doctor walked the length of the train distributing to the German wounded our ammunition, which he himself had broken to represent dum-dum.

Every time the train stopped this ammunition was shown to the infuriated public as dum-dum used by the English, and our guard would step aside to allow the mob to kick and loot us. Red Cross women fed the Germans at some of these halts, and frequently they would come into our truck and jeer at us. Occasionally one would greet us with 'Englishmen, are you thirsty ?' And pouring out some liquid would throw it in our faces. I have never known a train have so many or such long halts. I felt as if I would die of thirst.

Several English did die during the early part of the journey, but fortunately the conditions improved slightly as we approached Germany. After fifty hours' travelling, Lieutenant Nicholson, wounded in the spine, and myself were so bad that we were put out at Dortmund. We were sorry to leave our friends in distress, but extremely glad to finish this awful train journey.

Before the war I had never contemplated the possibility of capture, and the question as to how prisoners would be treated simply had not occurred to me. At the Marne we had captured four German officers and five hundred men, and it had been impossible to evacuate them for two days. During this period the rank and file had received the same rations as our men, and the officers fed as guests in our officers' mess. They were quite a good lot and I think appreciated the consideration. At halts during the advance to the Aisne it was quite a common sight to see small detachments of prisoners marched to the rear. Our men used frequently to throw them bits of our own rations and cigarettes. 'Fritz' as a prisoner was looked on as an object of pity, and some one to be treated with a certain amount of respect; after all, he had, at any rate, done his duty for his country, and our fighting soldiers did not harbour any personal feeling of hatred towards him.

This made it all the more difficult to understand the treatment we were receiving. I do not think it natural for any civilised human being to show such brutality. Later I formed the opinion that this treatment was part of a regular organised scheme to terrorise the world with a view to coercing neighbouring States to enter the war on the side of the Central Powers.

From the station at Dortmund we were taken to the 'Krankenhaus Barmherzigen Brüder.' Here we were met by the head Brother, one of the finest specimens of the human race that I have ever come across.

Seeing how bad we were and not having any place in his hospital for British officers, he had us put into bath-chairs and wheeled to his own private room, which was hastily prepared for us.

I was seven weeks in this hospital, and found the medical attention excellent. There appeared to be no limit to the kindness of the head Brother.

Once we were hurriedly removed from our comfortable room and put into a very much smaller one. We were told it was because two German officers were visiting the place. These two were very young doctors, who had been taken prisoner by the French but had been released as soon as all the wounded in the front line had been attended to.

They were typical Prussians. Our new room was far too good for English prisoners—we were to be moved out of it. All our books and other comforts were to be taken away. These were actually removed in their presence. Our meals were not to be served on plates, nor were we to have knives and forks, as the French had not given these luxuries to German prisoners in the front line. Our next meal was of a very inferior quality and was served on an inverted basin.

The following day, when these two Prussians had left Dortmund, we were put back into the head Brother's room again and everything that had been removed from us was returned.

Some German wounded were allowed to visit us, and all were pleasant, but naturally very full of the German successes. Our most objectionable visitor was an English lady, married to a German. It seemed to give her great pleasure to narrate all the atrocities perpetrated by England and tell us how ashamed she was of the country of her birth.

The head Brother will always stand out in my memory as a most remarkable man. His hospital, intended solely for Germans, was overcrowded, and he was obviously working under great difficulties. Besides us two officers, he had six or eight other prisoners, and all received every consideration. We always welcomed his visits, as he tried to cheer us up as much as he could, and later, when our letters from home started to arrive, it seemed to give him great pleasure to bring them to us himself.

Owing to the different opinions which exist as to whether it is right or not for a prisoner of war to try and escape, I will here state my own feelings on the subject.

For a month or six weeks it was out of the question for me to make any attempt owing to my wounds; but before I left that hospital there was absolutely nothing to prevent my walking out of the place, except the feeling that it was hardly the way to return the kindness shown to me by this remarkable man. No one could have persuaded me to take advantage of his kindness in any way that might have got him into trouble.

At 6 a.m. on the 14th December 1914, an under-officer, armed to the teeth, arrived to escort me to Torgau, where I was told I would find all the other English prisoners.

On arrival I found only one Englishman, Captain Knight Bruce, Warwickshire Regiment. He had been wounded through the lung and was too ill to accompany the other English prisoners, who had been moved elsewhere about three weeks previously.

There were about five hundred Russians, and the same number of French and a few Belgians in this camp.

There are two fortresses in Torgau, and both were used as prisoner of war camps. I was brought to Fort Brückenkopf on the eastern bank of the Elbe. Built in the days of Napoleon, it was a small fortress about three hundred yards by two hundred yards entirely surrounded by a moat fifty yards wide and thirty feet deep. Three sides of the Fort consisted of ramparts thirty feet high. The fourth side was bounded by a wall, twenty feet high, and had three bridges, over the moat, leading on to a road along the flood bank of the Elbe. The moat was dry, but contained a high barbed-wire fence. At night the whole fort, both inside and outside, was brilliantly lit up by arc lamps. (See plan on page 84.)

A guard eighty strong with many dogs was accommodated in a building near the entrance gate and furnished sentries on both sides of the defences. The main building had accommodation for about a hundred and sixty prisoners in small rooms containing from two to twenty officers. The remaining prisoners were accommodated in wagon-sheds, or stables, where each room held from twenty to eighty.

As prisoners were not allowed to approach the ramparts the only view they could get beyond the four walls of the fortress was from a building known as the ' elevated abort with the western aspect.'

The conditions in the camp, though better than during the first few months of the war, were far from satisfactory, Only for a short time was I allowed to live in the same room as Knight Bruce. In January I was moved to the other end of the camp, where I shared a room with twenty French and twenty Russians. The beds were almost touching, and it was still necessary to have some placed on top of others. German barrack-room beds are so made that they can be fitted on top of each other, and sometimes for lack of space were piled three or four deep.

With a clerical staff of French officers administrative arrangements gradually improved.

By the time I reached Torgau, I had only partially recovered the use of my left hand, but thanks to the treatment I received from a qualified French masseur further progress was assured. Soon after the Christmas festivities, such as they were, I found myself frequently considering the possibility of escape.

To break out of the camp did not strike me as an impossibility, but without a knowledge of German I did not see how I could remain at large for more than a week or ten days, which would be nothing like sufficient time to reach any frontier on foot. There was no means of getting expert advice as to the minimum amount of food necessary to keep body and soul together for a cross-country walk of three or four hundred miles. I soon made friends with Lieut. Bourcier, a French artillery reserve officer, who had been attached to the 19th Hussars as interpreter. He spoke German fluently and was used by the authorities to do a lot of administrative work within the camp. He was very partial to the English and disliked the Germans, possibly more than any of us. I found him a ready listener to discuss possibilities of escape.

By the end of January, Bourcier had formed a definite plan. His employment in the camp brought him in touch with many German civilians ready for small bribes. He even succeeded in getting a photograph of himself in plain clothes taken inside the camp, this being necessary for the passport,

BOURCIER'S ESCAPE

which he forged. Although he intended to go by train the whole way to Denmark, he was quite prepared to bring me with him. With my very limited knowledge of German, I felt my presence would be courting disaster for both of us, and, in spite of his willingness, I firmly refused to prejudice his chance. Had I possessed then the confidence in myself which I afterwards acquired I believe we could have succeeded together.

In February 1915, disguised as a commercial traveller with samples collected from the various tradesmen with whom he had dealings, Bourcier walked out of the front gate one day, just showing the customary pass to the sentry.

When he was completely dressed ready to go, he asked me to stroll past the gate and stop to read some notices in that vicinity. My sole responsibility was to hang about in the neighbourhood of the gate so that in the event of early capture I could pick up and destroy his forged passport, which he would drop as he was being marched to the guard-room.

Humble as my part was, I remember standing there with shaking knees, thinking what a wonderful nerve Bourcier had. In a week he reached London. He sent me a very nice parcel from Denmark, which was the first news I received of his success.

In March two French officers, at a certain amount of personal risk, effected an escape one night. They walked thirty kilometres and then surrendered themselves to a priest because they were hungry. On return to Torgau they imagined they were tremendous heroes, and took the greatest pride in explaining every detail of their wonderful escape to the commandant.

The authorities, of course, at once took additional steps to safeguard the camp against similar efforts.

I had by now collected quite a number of stores and had made up my mind to try my luck at walking to the frontier alone, there being no one in the camp who would accompany me. I still had hopes of being able to get out of the camp, but was just waiting for slightly warmer weather.

In April 1915 Lieut. Templer, Gloucestershire Regiment, arrived with six very fine Russian officers. They had escaped from their previous camp and had been seven days in the country, living on about half a stick of chocolate a day, before being recaptured. It was most interesting for me to get first-hand evidence of life in the country from the escaper's point of view.

Templer was a cadet at Sandhurst when war was declared, and was wounded and taken prisoner in December 1914, so he had not wasted much time over his first attempt. He was suffering now from poisoning in his legs caused by barbed wire in his final action in France.

He was kept in bed in a room used as a hospital inside the camp, where I used to visit him frequently and get all the information I could. Here I met one of his Russian friends, a very young colonel. In the Russo-Japanese War this man had been wounded and captured at Port Arthur. Before his capture then he had been twice through the Japanese lines with important dispatches and he had subsequently escaped from the Japanese.

What luck to find a man with such wonderful experience.

The colonel wasted no time in organising an escape from Torgau. Templer, noticing my enthusiasm, roped me in, as they had just room for one more.

A vast sum of money was required for two heavy bribes. One to a German employed inside the camp, who was going to conduct us along a secret exit, while a sentry who was a pal of his was on duty at the other end; the other to a German Jew, a smuggler on a large scale by trade, who was prepared to drive us in two powerful motor-cars to either the Dutch or Swiss frontier and hand us over there to his agent. He frequently did these journeys by road and anticipated little risk of recapture.

I cannot remember the exact sum required, but both insisted on being paid cash in advance. The best terms we could agree to were, when all was ready we would pay the man inside, who would take us to where the Jew would be waiting with the two cars, and then we would pay the latter.

It was absolutely out of the question for us to get all the money required, so trading on the fact that all is fair in love and war, we decided to collect enough for the first man, and when we were outside offer the second a promissory note and just seize his cars if he refused. We had two mechanics in our party, but we did not expect a refusal, as the Jew most certainly would have been shot had we given him away.

I wrote a cheque for as large a sum as my bank

balance would stand, and bribed another German employed in the camp to go to Holland to cash it. To get this done I had to pay seventy-five per cent commission.

By the middle of May, we had collected sufficient money and clothes. Our Jew was confident of reaching either frontier, but we feared the bridges on the roads to Holland might be watched if news of our escape was made known, so decided to make for Switzerland. Almost on the even of departure Italy came into the war, and our Jew fearing additional precautions might be taken on the Swiss frontier, though still agreeable to take us there, suggested it might now be wiser to go to Holland. We quite agreed and gave him four days in which to make the necessary arrangements with his agent there. It was during these four days that a large fire broke out in the camp, necessitating the immediate removal of a hundred and fifty prisoners. Although none of us lived in the burnt building our names appeared amongst those to go. We were looked on as undesirables—Templer and the Russians because they had already escaped, and myself because I had previously been awarded a short term of imprisonment for failing to salute a German officer.

Our new destination, Burg-bei-Magdeburg, was completely deserted when we arrived on the 2nd June 1915. So easy for an escape did this camp appear at first sight that our hopes were in no way shattered. It was surrounded by a wooden fence eight feet high with several strands of barbed wire on top and a high barbed wire fence five yards outside.

The very next day the Russians started on a tunnel from a room beside the guard-room. Finding water there during the first week they immediately started another at the opposite side of the camp. This they expected to complete in three weeks, coming out into a cornfield. The tunnel progressed at a fair rate until it was within a week of completion. The Russians then noticed that one of their number, who had been marched into the camp a few days after our arrival, was frequently talking to the Germans. This man shared a room on the first story with some of our party. As none of the Russians knew anything about this officer, they decided to hold a court martial on him one night in his own room. There they managed to elicit the information that he was a German, and had been sent into the camp as a spy, that he was telling the Germans all details about the tunnel, and that they were going to wait at the mouth and shoot us like rabbits as we emerged. The Russians then sentenced him to death as an enemy spy wearing their uniform. They arranged to carry out the sentence immediately by erecting a scaffold and hanging him. In desperation the spy asked for five minutes in which to say his prayers, when he suddenly hurled himself through the closed window and was believed to have broken his neck. I saw no more of those Russians, as they were at once removed for a long term of imprisonment. I occupied a room with Templer and one other English officer. Soon the remaining twenty beds were filled up by the release of the officers who had been in prison as a reprisal for captured German submarine crews being sent to detention barracks in England.

I then met Captain Cartwright, of the Middlesex Regiment, for the first time as a prisoner. We were in the same Brigade on the outbreak of war, occupied the same barracks at Devonport, and had been at Sandhurst and Malvern together.

Little did I realise then what the future had in store for both of us.

II

BURG

By H. A. CARTWRIGHT

Captured at Mons—Journey to Germany—Torgau—At Burg—Plans for escape—In the civil jail—Camp spies—Clothes for escape—Planning a route—Tailoring and dyeing operations—A fiasco—Walking out of Burg camp with Harrison—Nine days of freedom—Recapture at Rostock—Journey back to Burg—The Germans as searchers—Removal to Halle and Torgau.

THE foregoing chapter affords all that is necessary by way of introduction to the events which it is the object of this book to describe, and my experience at the front being of the shortest, I will therefore bring my own story down to the same point in the fewest possible words.

I crossed to Boulogne with my battalion on 12th-13th August 1914. After a ten days' picnic in ideal weather among a friendly peasant population we suddenly and rather unexpectedly met the enemy before Mons on the 23rd, in the first action of the war.

We were very heavily engaged and the 'fog of war' was at its thickest when my half company went into action a little later than the rest of the battalion. By the early afternoon the battalion had suffered terribly, and the remnant of my company was almost completely isolated when I tried to enter a cottage to see if I could get a view from its upper windows. Whether I got in or not I do not know, for the cottage and I were mixed up together in the burst of a shell, and thereafter my recollections are of the haziest. I do not think I was knocked out for long, but it was long enough for me to be seen by a man who got away and reached home with the first batch of wounded, where he favoured my friends and relations with a detailed and gruesome account of the manner of my death. At about 6 or 7 p.m. I was hiding in a ditch with some half dozen more or less wounded men—with hordes of Germans moving about all round us—praying for darkness or the counter-attack, which we confidently expected although the sounds of firing were becoming always more and more distant, when we were captured by German reserves, who had not been in action at all. (Remember the optimism of 1914—that something had gone wrong locally was only too clear, but that the whole British Expeditionary Force had been overwhelmed and driven back was unimaginable !)

The next day we began the march towards Germany, being joined at intervals by other parties of prisoners which brought our numbers to about two hundred men with five officers. On the whole we were well treated (but with notable exceptions, especially when we came in contact with non-combatants), though the only food we got was what was given us by the civil population. A few farm wagons were commandeered and the more severely wounded—with the fattest German under-officers—were allowed to ride in them. I was continually questioned by intelligence officers, but most of them accepted civilly enough my refusal to give any information except my name and rank. Some blustered and bullied. One major produced a pistol and threatened to blow my brains out, and so worked himself up that I think he would have done it had not a young German officer who had been at an English public school come to the rescue.

We arrived at Louvain at dusk of the 26th August and found half the town in flames, parties of soldiers busy setting fire to more houses and indiscriminate firing going on in all directions. There was a good deal of drunkenness among the Germans. We were crowded into one room of the cavalry barracks for the night. Early next morning we were hurriedly marched out of the barracks and told that the rest of the town would be destroyed as a reprisal for the operations of *francs-tireurs* during the night. One man and two horses of our escort had, they said, been killed actually in the barracks, and they certainly had two dead horses to support the story. We were marched to the station yard through wrecked streets of burning and looted houses and shops, with here and there the corpse of a civilian lying where it had fallen. As soon as we arrived at the station a battery of field howitzers, drawn up close to the line, opened fire and continued the work of destruction.

The station buildings were the headquarters of the general officer commanding the railhead and surrounding district. The guard and sentries outside them were in an appalling state of nerves and fired continually, apparently at anything that moved in the wrecked town around them.

We stood in the station yard for five or six hours, and during this time parties of soldiers kept arriving and bringing with them civilian prisoners, mostly old men and youths, though there were one or two women among them, with their hands tied behind them. More than once we saw prisoners led out of the station to the back of a goods shed, heard volleys and saw the guards return without them.

At about 2 p.m. we entrained and began a journey which dragged out for seventy-two hours before we detrained at Sennelager, a sort of German Aldershot, in Westphalia. During the journey—and near the end of it—we were given one very light meal, and the only other food we got was what the escort were able to collect beyond their own needs from the Red Cross women who handed them food and drink at some of the bigger stations—with strict injunctions not to give any to us.

We were about ten days at Sennelager, where we were joined by some thirty more British officers, several hundred men, and a few Belgians. While there I was able to get off a telegram, by some roundabout means which I have forgotten, to the

British Consul-General at Rotterdam asking him to inform my relations that I was alive. I also gave a small cheque to the German Red Cross, writing under my signature the words 'Please inform next-of-kin.' The cheque beat the telegram by a week.

We were left pretty much to ourselves at Sennelager, and the only memorable incident was when a Belgian officer's attempt to visit a latrine by night caused the sentries to open fire in all directions, and one of them was severely wounded.

'*Paris gefallen!*' was the daily cry of the sentries and of the civilians who crowded round the camp to get a look at us.

About September 10th all the British officers were moved to Torgau, where we were joined by most of the officers taken at the Aisne and by all the French officers from Maubeuge.

It was here that the first attempt to escape was made by a British officer. I don't think I ever knew exactly what his plans were, but I know that they were thoroughly thought out and that, knowing the language well, he had a good chance of success. A day or two later he was reported by the Germans to be dead, but they gave no satisfactory explanation of the circumstances of his death, which, as far as I know, were never cleared up.

In the middle of December the camp at Torgau was broken up and I was sent with about fifty other British officers to Burg-bei-Magdeburg.

Burg is six hundred kilometres from the Swiss frontier and four hundred from Holland. The camp had been hastily formed by throwing a fence round a group of gun-sheds and mobilisation store-rooms. We English—all bagged at Mons and Le Cateau—were a small minority in a large mob of Belgian, Russian and French officers. A few rank and file of all nations were kept in the camp for fatigue duties.

It was early in 1915, when it had become quite evident that the war was not going to be a matter of a month or two, that a few of us first began to discuss the possibility of escape, and about the middle of February I began with another British officer seriously to work out a plan.

We decided that it would be quite possible, as soon as the weather became warmer, to walk to the Dutch frontier, travelling always by night and lying hidden in the forests by day. Neither of us could speak a word of German so a train journey was out of the question.

We bought, from a peddling bookseller who was allowed to visit the camp, a North German Baedeker which contained a few maps, and, from a study of these, though they did not cover the whole route, it seemed that the road was not too difficult. There appeared to be plenty of woods and forests.

We decided to collect a store of chocolate, biscuits, oxo and other portable forms of food from the parcels which were then beginning to arrive, believing that we could carry enough of such concentrated foods for a month's walk. We counted on being able to steal a certain amount of roots, etc., to give the necessary bulk. We thought that we should be able, without much risk, to light fires for cooking purposes in the woods.

At this time we had no experience of any sort on which to build, and there was a good deal of scepticism shown by the majority of prisoners as to the possibility of walking several hundred miles through a hostile country without coming in contact with anyone or buying food on the way. During the last three years of the war, however, nearly all the successful escapes were made in this way.

The camp was very strongly fenced and guarded, so we came to the conclusion that the best chance of getting out was to make a tunnel, starting in one of the camp buildings and finishing in an allotment field about twenty yards outside the fence. We wanted two more workers so invited a Sapper to join us, thinking that his expert knowledge would be helpful. He immediately flattened us out by a long, technical dissertation on tunnelling, pointing out that we should have no less than thirty tons of earth to dispose of, that we should require all sorts of tools and that we must have specially constructed frames, which could be taken into the tunnel in sections and there fitted together, to support the roof, etc., etc., etc. I mention this because I think it is of interest in view of later experiences. I myself know of eight tunnels which were successful, two of them more than a hundred yards long, and many more which were unsuccessful only through their being given away by spies, while I know of only one which fell in, or rather gave way, under the weight of an enormous German sentry.

Probably the Sapper's calculation of the amount of earth to be got rid of was correct (for a tunnel of three foot square section—the prisoner was generally content with a two-foot section), but three or four times that amount of earth must have been removed in tunnelling at other camps. As much as possible was generally packed beneath the room where the tunnel started—and other 'well disposed' rooms—and the remainder was carried out in pockets and small bags and thrown into latrine pits or scattered about the exercise grounds.

Tools were easily made from odds and ends of wood, table knives, parts of barrack beds and the variegated scrap material with which any place considered good enough for officer prisoners was generally littered. At least one tunnel was ventilated by a prisoner-made air-pump and tubing and several were lit by electricity—from the camp mains. Roofing and props were made from bed-boards, roof-linings, the flooring of empty rooms and any other wood which might be handy. When the German missed woodwork he always took it for granted that it had been used to supplement the very meagre coal ration which he handed out. If there happened to be no tunnelling in progress he was right.

After this set-back—for we naturally believed the expert—we began to look for another way out of the camp, without at first hitting on any plan with a decent chance of success.

These first schemings ended when I was sent to the local civil jail, with seven other British officers, by way of reprisal for the internment of German submarine crews in detention barracks in England. Solitary confinement, after several months in a very small room in which three Russians, three Frenchmen, three Belgians and only one other Englishman slept, cooked, ate, quarrelled, spat and sometimes washed their feet, was the purest bliss. The story of our life in Burg jail, the kindness of the prison staff, who stoutly asserted that we had committed no crime and flatly refused to treat us as criminals, and the trouble and risks which they took to defeat the intentions of the commandant—a Hun of Huns—would fill a small book, but it would be quite out of place in this account.

Escape from the prison would have been a fairly easy matter, but no one else there (except one man who was trying to organise outside help with the aid of friends at home) believed at that time in the possibility of getting clear of the country, and I certainly did not feel inclined to attempt that long walk alone.

I came out of prison in June 1915 and returned to Burg camp, which I found much enlarged. All the prisoners whom I had known had gone to other camps, and a new batch, of whom only three were English, had been brought in. Among them was Charles Harrison, of the Royal Irish Regiment, whom I had never previously met, although we had been at school and Sandhurst together and our battalions had occupied and mobilised in the same barracks at Devonport.

Harrison one day found me making a copy of a 'camp permit,' a small printed ticket which was given to contractors and workmen who visited the camp and which was supposed to be given up to the guard on their leaving. I was making the permit without having any definite idea as to how it might be used, but I had always at the back of my mind the feeling that the easiest way out was through the front door. Harrison told me that he meant to try to escape, and we decided to work together. As later events showed, he was by far the most ingenious, resourceful and determined trier of all those who eventually turned their hands to the business.

The first important discovery which we made was of the absolute necessity of keeping our own counsel and not telling a soul about our plans until it was necessary to ask for help. The desirability of this was proved shortly afterwards when two Russian tunnels were given away to the Germans, and the Russians caught out, as a spy, one of their own people. The man was disguised as an officer but had never been in their army at all. A Belgian soldier was also clearly proved to be giving information to the camp adjutant.

A word on the subject of spies and their kind may not be out of place here, since a few of them were provided gratis in all the Prussian camps which I visited, except Küstrin. As well as the Russian pseudo-officer mentioned above I knew of two others of the same nationality who were certainly spies (posing as officers), but who were not found out until their disappearance from their camps coincided with the exposure of large-scale, mad, Russian plans for breaking out. I heard of many others in camps which I did not visit. In one camp there was an English (half Hun) civilian who was very strongly suspected; the reasons given for his not being in Ruhleben—the civilians' camp—were unconvincing. A child of five would not have trusted him, and he had no sort of success. In another camp an alleged French priest fell under suspicion, but I left that camp and never heard what became of him.

German *agents provocateurs* were much more common. They generally followed some nominal employment in the *Kommandantur* which necessitated their coming and going constantly among the prisoners. I never heard of their trapping an Englishman, but they scored heavily among the other nationalities, especially the Russians, many of whom could never resist the opportunity of possessing a forbidden article, no matter how useless, or of obtaining liquor, whether it was forbidden or not. There was never any originality about the *agents'* procedure; they always opened the ball by offering to buy something that was forbidden or to secure the dispatch of an uncensored letter or parcel.

In Magdeburg jail one of the German orderlies, an excessively dirty little Polish Jew, pestered us at all hours with offers of anything from automatic pistols to women. We told the adjutant that we didn't want any of the commodities offered and would be grateful if he would provide an *agent* who stank less, but he only threatened more courts martial, and the little beast continued unabashed to offer his services.

On one occasion Harrison and I heard two British officers, who, leaning against the window of the interpreters' office, were discussing our plans at the tops of their voices.

I mention these details because they show how greatly our difficulties were increased by the necessity of secrecy, not only from the Germans, but from every one inside the camp.

The Burg camp (see plan on page 36), was bounded all round by a fence of solid boarding about eight feet high with six strands of overhung barbed wire on the top. Outside this was a twenty-strand barbed wire fence about ten feet high—in all about thirty-one miles of wire were used for a perimeter of six hundred yards. There was one sentry—or more—at every angle outside, and sentries inside at every point where buildings stood close to the board fence. There were big arc lights dotted about all over the inside and small electric lamps at about twenty-yard intervals along the board fence.

The exits were, firstly, a small gate giving on to the road just by the guard-room, where a lot of idle German soldiers were always loafing; and, secondly, close to it, a big double gate for wagons. All civilians had to pass through the small gate, showing a pass, and all soldiers were supposed to do the same, but there was a good deal of slackness in the carrying out of these rules.

We decided that the only way out was through one of the gates, and accordingly we began to work on two alternative plans so as to have something to fall back upon if anything should occur to upset one of them.

One plan was to wait for a wet day, when the guard and loafers would be inside the guard-room, disguise ourselves as workmen and try to shuffle out with sacks over our heads (a common practice in wet weather), carrying a stove between us with several lengths of stove-piping. We should show the permits, which I was making, as we passed the gate. The advantage of this plan was that we could stow any amount of food, extra clothing, rucksacks, etc., in the stove and pipes and re-pack at leisure when we got into cover outside the camp. The attempt was to be made just before dusk, and we knew of cover within a few hundred yards of the gate.

The other plan was to disguise ourselves as German officers and walk straight out of the gate. This also would have to be just at dusk, so that we should

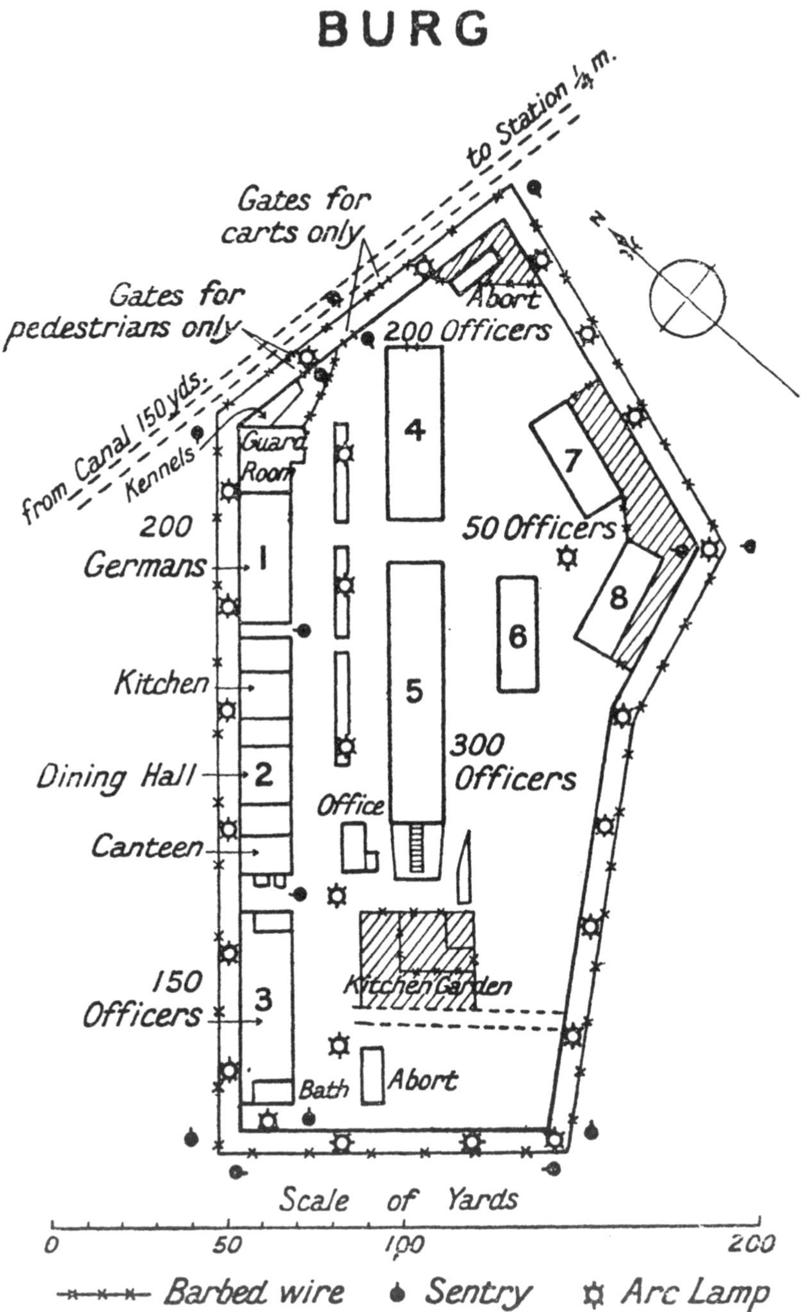
BURG
to Station ¼ m.
Gates for
carts only
Gates for
pedestrians only
from Canal 150 yds.
Kennels
Guard Room
Abort
200 Officers
4
7
50 Officers
200
Germans
1
8
6
Kitchen
5
300
Officers
Dining Hall
2
Office
Canteen
150
Officers
3
Kitchen Garden
Bath
Abort
Scale of Yards
0
50
100
200
Barbed wire
Sentry
Arc Lamp
Out of Bounds
1 - 5 Mobilization Store buildings
6 - 8 Wooden Huts

soon have darkness to cover our change of clothes; but it must be light enough for us to be easily recognised as officers.

We were prepared to gamble on no Hun soldier daring to address an officer who failed to show a pass, no matter how strict or intricate the rules on the subject might be.

For this plan we needed German officers' great-coats, caps, leggings and swords—or something that looked very like them. I apologise for the following long description of our uniform, but to us the matter was of the first importance.

Harrison wrote to his tailor, told him that he was being transferred to the Grenadiers and ordered the great-coat of that regiment, which is of a blue-grey colour instead of the universal drab. I asked a Grenadier of about my own build to order a coat for me. Harrison also ordered from his tailor two blue caps with red bands—the undress cap of his regiment—which, with a little card-board stuffing, could be made to look exactly like the German home-service cap. The German wears two small badges on his cap; they consist of, in Prussia, small silver rings with, in the top one, a red spot in the middle, and, in the bottom one, a silver Maltese cross on a black ground. Each is mounted on a rosette of patent leather. With buttons and silver paper I made badges which would have passed any inspection, notwithstanding the fact that the red spots were really minute Union

Jacks and the Maltese crosses were spread-eagle angels of peace. We made this little variation because we were not too happy as to how the Germans might view the wearing of their uniform by enemies in the event of our recapture, and preferred to be able to deny that what we were wearing was their uniform at all; but we have since often wondered what the infuriated Germans would have thought had they caught us wearing what appeared to be German uniform with a Union Jack on the cap!

The shoulder-straps were more difficult. They consist each of two pieces of silver braid, curled round a button and mounted on cloth of various colours, according to the corps, regiment, etc. They carry badges of rank, numerals and sometimes regimental badges. I made the braid by weaving blue, grey and white silk on a kind of Heath Robinson loom, and the effect was a good enough imitation of silver. Later the German took to making his shoulder-straps, for active service, of silk instead of silver, so ours were not only effective but correct. We bought stars (they were much like our own pattern) and numerals and plain gilt buttons (as worn by all ranks) at the camp canteen. On a show of worn-out boots—borrowed without leave from a Belgian private—we were allowed to buy new yellow boots, and we bought yellow leggings from the merchant who came to supply them. Harrison carved the swords very artistically out of bits of packing-case. The German service-dress scabbard is of black metal, so we blackened the last eighteen inches of them, which was as much as would show below our great-coats, and polished them with boot-blacking.

While waiting for our great-coats we began to work out a route.

The Swiss frontier was ruled out by distance.

At this time nothing was known of the Dutch frontier by anyone in the camp, but we imagined that it was very closely guarded, and possibly wired, and we thought it probable that the whole frontier district would be very carefully supervised and controlled.

We knew, from watching the comic 'alarms' which the Commandant was in the habit of staging, that cyclist patrols would be sent out on all likely roads as soon as any prisoner was missed, and we thought it likely that towns and villages lying west of the camp would be on the look-out. For these reasons, and on account of many other difficulties, possibly quite imaginary, which our complete ignorance of conditions in Germany may have made us exaggerate, we decided to go north to the Baltic.

Not till daylight on the morning after we were missed was the 'alarm' given a genuine trial. Then with all the prisoners craning from the windows of their rooms, the Commandant himself dispatched his patrols, giving them suitable advice in a loud harangue. Police dogs, the things now called Alsatians, were produced, our bedding was brought out, and they were invited to take up the trail from it. They were interested in the bedding neither more nor less than they would have been in a lamp-post.

We decided to go first to Rostock, whence we believed there was a daily service of ferry-boats into Denmark. As a matter of fact we were wrong; the ferries ran from Warnemünde, at the mouth of the Warne, fifteen kilometres north of Rostock.

We thought it might be possible to board a ferry at night, stow ourselves away and so cross into Denmark. Failing this, rumour had it that there were many small sailing-boats about the Baltic coast engaged in smuggling cheese, butter, etc., into Germany. We thought we might find one of these and persuade the skipper to take us across. If we found a Dane all would probably go smoothly; if a German, ten months in the Fatherland had shown us that the conscience-price of the average working-class German was very dear at fifty marks, and we had about two hundred between us. Thirdly, there was always the possibility of finding a boat on the beach and rowing or sailing it across. We were neither of us experienced sailors, but the distance was not much over twenty miles, and we had only to steer approximately northwards and we could not fail to hit Denmark somewhere. We gathered that, owing to the shortage of food, which was beginning to be seriously felt, and the consequent desirability of getting as much Danish produce as possible into the country, the customs' officers did not unnecessarily worry the masters of fishing or small trading vessels, and were not too severe in their visits to the ferries and other small steamers, though they kept, of course, a very strict watch for spies on the docks and in the town.

Apropos the question of bribery, a few words on the German soldier as I found him may not be out of place here. After nearly twelve years I have come to the conclusion that he was not, on the average, a bad fellow. The swine among them were such incredibly swinish swine that for some years it was difficult to realise that the swine were a small minority.

More often than not the camp guards and escorts tried to do their job, and to do it without being unnecessarily offensive. I do not include the sergeant-majors or other senior N.C.O.'s or the office staffs, which were composed principally of ex-waiters, shopkeepers and commercial travellers, and were about ninety-nine per cent swine; nearly all those who were not swine found pleasanter, if more dangerous jobs, than looking after prisoners.

Most of the swinish acts of soldiers which I saw, both in Germany and in Belgium in 1914, were done under the direct orders or incitement of officers.

The rank and file were corrupt in a small way, but only in accordance with the custom of the country, and I doubt if many of them would have accepted money to help a prisoner to escape.

Probably most of them would have taken the money and reported the prisoner or sought kudos and promotion by waiting for him and shooting him in the act—as was actually done on at least one occasion. Anyhow, it wasn't a game worth risking. They couldn't resist food, but when, by accepting it, they were assisting the plans of a prisoner they did so, probably, from sheer stupidity. Their stupidity was incredible.

There were of course revolutionary socialists who were given jobs in camps because they could not be trusted anywhere else, and their kind would do anything for money; but no prisoner ever risked trusting them in an actual attempt to escape.

Rostock was due north of us and distant a little more than two hundred kilometres (a hundred and twenty-five miles) as the crow flies—to which must be added about twenty-five per cent to get the distance as the prisoner treks. The road, as far as we could tell from Baedeker, was nearly straight, and one of the Baedeker maps covered a little more than half the distance. We got the names of a couple of small towns which lay on our line, beyond the limits of the map, from a small-scale map of Europe which was sold as a war map. We stole a compass from a brother officer, who, by some oversight, had not been deprived of it on his capture. We must give him a new one some day.

We hoped to start about the last week in September, when the nights would be fairly long and the weather not too cold. We did not reckon, however, on the imbecility of tailors.

Since June we had been walking ten or twelve miles a day, very fast, round and round the exercise ground.

Early in September our ' workmen ' scheme was knocked on the head by the Germans so wiring off the small gate that no one could approach it without passing through the guard-room (see plan on page 36). This was more than we could face. At the same time the rule that no civilian might pass out by the wagon gate was strictly enforced.

These precautions were due to the escape of a Belgian, who walked out of the camp during a thunderstorm disguised as a female Hun cook. His line of departure had been a complete mystery to the camp authorities, but on re-capture the next day he had told them how it was done, so the net result of his efforts was to queer our pitch.

There remained the ' officer ' scheme.

The first hitch in this took the shape of a post-card from Harrison's tailor saying that he was sending off the great-coat, but suggesting that Harrison had made a mistake in asking for the caps of his old regiment when he must have meant the Grenadiers' cap.

Harrison, however, managed to bluff the censors into allowing him to send off a post card immediately —without the usual fourteen days' delay which was the rule in all the camps—asking his tailor not to try to think but to do what he was told. The delay in the censor's office was intended to ensure that any secret information sent by prisoners' post should arrive stale. It also gave the censors time to test at leisure for all kinds of invisible ink. Harrison was allowed to dispatch this card at once, as the camp rule was: 'Prisoners must always wear headgear so as to be able to salute German officers.' He always went about bare-headed, claiming he had no head-dress, and had been ordered to write home for a uniform cap. The reply from the tailor was sufficient to justify an extra card to expedite dispatch.

Then the Grenadier who had ordered a coat for me was transferred to another camp, and, although he tried to arrange for me to have the opening of the parcel containing the coat when it came to Burg, the censors somehow muddled things and I never got it.

I therefore began to negotiate with an old Russian colonel for a cape which he had had made by a German tailor, and which, while it was, presumably, something like the cape of his regiment, was exactly the cut and colour of the German article in all respects, except that it had no red-lined collar. After weeks of haggling I persuaded the old man to part with the garment in exchange for a 'British Warm,' a large sum of money and a promise that, if I were caught and the cape traced to him, I would swear that I had stolen it. He was a confirmed drunkard, and we hated his knowing anything about the scheme, but I had to have his cape.

Harrison's great-coat and the caps arrived together on 5th November. Everything else had been ready for some weeks.

Having had no sample in the camp from which to judge, we had rather banked on the Grenadier great-coat bearing a strong resemblance to the German article, but we found to our horror that it was entirely different both in cut and colour. The former is a thoroughly serviceable, comfortable garment of a dark slatey-blue grey, while the latter is almost as tight as a frock-coat, of a lightish blue colour, and is covered with flaps and buttons. We had been quite prepared to add the flaps and buttons, and we had hoped that the difference in colour would be so slight as hardly to matter in a bad light, but we had not contemplated any dyeing or extensive and complicated tailoring. However, there was nothing for it but to start in on the job.

The tailoring which we had to do could not be done with any sort of secrecy in the crowded room in which Harrison and I lived, but Elliot, of Harrison's regiment, who had a small room to himself in a hut barrack (Block 7 on plan), very kindly allowed us to use it as a workshop, and here for a time we worked undisturbed. But, just as the coat and cape began to look unmistakably German, the room was suddenly raided by a gang of under-officers, who arrested Elliot, on some trumped-up charge of bribery, and proceeded to search the room. We managed to shuffle our gear out of the window, which was fortunately open, and, not being ourselves 'wanted,' got clear of the room in the general mess-up and retrieved everything unharmed. Elliot's arrest was the work of the Belgian informer, mentioned earlier in the note on his kind, who had been hanging around the room for some days without, however, being able to discover what was going on. He had been assisted by a Polish Jew, in the uniform of a Russian Red Cross orderly, who had offered to supply Elliot with anything from brandy to machine-guns, and had been very unkindly rebuffed.

We went on with the work in another small room in a similar hut.

Three or four days after the arrival of the coat the tailoring was complete. We then laid it on the floor and poured over it about a pound of boracic powder, the only white powder available, which we beat into the cloth with brushes. This rather crude treatment had the desired effect of raising the shade of the coat to a much lighter blue—a bit patchy, but good enough in a bad light.

We first dressed for the attempt on the 10th November. We wore double or treble the usual allowance of underclothes and numerous sweaters, cardigans, etc. I had an old Norfolk jacket, acquired in hospital by a British officer who had lost his uniform. Harrison had a uniform jacket.

dipped in ink, from which the pockets, flaps, shoulder-straps, etc., had been removed. We both wore corduroy trousers with thin red stripes down the seams, this being the only kind of nether garment which we were allowed to buy to replace our worn-out uniforms. We painted out the stripes with water-colour.

Our food, which consisted of chocolate, biscuits, potted meat, 'Bivouac' cocoa, beef tabloids, malted milk, oxo, etc., with a 'Tommy's cooker' and supply of solid spirit (all from home parcels) was packed all over our bodies. Some was in pockets and some down trouser legs, some in rucksacks hung over our stomachs and some in sacks hung on our backsides. The latter two loads gave the correct Prussian figure.

I had for months past worn a long, straggling moustache; I hogged this closely and mounted a pair of enormous round gold-rimmed spectacles. Harrison is very fair, so his moustache, eyebrows and back hair were blacked with grease-paint (the kindly Hun provided this for a purely imaginary dramatic club) and his face was washed in a strong solution of coffee. These alterations changed our appearance enough to make recognition unlikely in a bad light, but they were, as things turned out, quite wasted.

Our outer garments consisted of the uniform caps, the great-coat in Harrison's case, the cape in mine, yellow boots and leggings, and the correct brown leather gloves. We wore our wooden swords.

Since I should have to discard my cape when we were safely out of the camp, I wore beneath it a Belgian army great-coat (dark blue) deprived of its frills and with civilian buttons. I had to pin up the skirts to prevent them from showing beneath the cape.

Harrison's German overcoat could be hastily converted into a seedy-looking civilian garment—most of the powder would soon wear out of it and we did not intend to be seen, as civilians, by daylight.

We intended to loiter in the darkness of a doorway near the wagon gate, until the departure of a kitchen refuse wagon which went out nearly every evening at about the right time. Then, when the gate was opened we hoped to be able to strut through it without attracting undue attention. Strange German officers often visited the camp on mysterious missions to the Russians, so that, if they accepted us at all as officers, the guard were not likely to pay much attention to us.

The German officer's collar, when turned up, shows a deep lining of scarlet cloth. This splash of red marks out the officer very clearly at any distance at which the colour can be seen, and the German soldier who sees it coming either bolts for cover or, if too late, shakes himself together for a terrific salute.

Lieutenant Terlinden, a Belgian officer of Guides, who afterwards brought off a particularly neat escape and sent me a lot of valuable information and material from Holland, sacrificed his breeches to provide our red collars.

We reached our doorway (in Block 4—see plan on page 36) safely, wearing English great-coats on top of all the rest. One British officer carried our caps while another lounged outside reporting German movements and watching for the wagon.

Just as the wagon hove in sight and our quick change was being effected, two German under-officers elected to loaf into our particular doorway, where they stood, talking about food, but not for the moment taking any great interest in us. This was not on the programme. Our group broke up in some disorder, but, after dodging all over the camp and meeting an unexpected German (all of them, fortunately, stone-blind) at every turn, we eventually reached our rooms with the loss of only one cap-badge.

After this fiasco we had to change our tactics. Secrecy was no longer possible, since half the officers in the camp knew now what we were at, and any unusual movement of Britishers attracted a mob of chattering allies. We decided to wait in my room (in Block 5—see plan on page 36), which I shared with five other British officers until the wagon was signalled, when we would walk out of it, along a corridor, down a staircase and across about a hundred yards of exercise ground to the gate. We hoped to time our start so as to reach the gate just as it was being opened. We took the precaution of smashing the electric lamps in the corridor and on the stairs, in case we should meet a German on our way down.

A little diversion, in the shape of a fire-alarm, was arranged for the guard in case any of them should think too much, after our departure, of the two strange officers who had walked out by the wagon gate. This was to be the burning of a large range of wooden latrines, and Bevan, of the Intelligence Corps, very kindly undertook to be the incendiary.

Large quantities of paper were thrown into the pit, and half a dozen large bottles of methylated spirit, which we could at that time buy in unlimited quantities for cooking purposes, were poured on to it. Bevan was to carelessly drop a match as soon as we were safely past the last sentry, and we felt sure that the subject of fire would crowd all other thoughts from the minds of the camp staff and guard for some hours at least.

We dressed for an attempt on 11th November, but it was dark before the wagon appeared. The same thing happened on 12th and 13th. On 13th a German officer came into the room while we were waiting, and we had to dive into very insufficient cover under a bed and a table while he stood within a few inches of Harrison asking silly questions about Irish politics. This sort of thing was more than I had bargained for, and, although Harrison was quite willing to dress up every night until our chance came, the thing was getting on my nerves, and I was afraid of doing something idiotic and spoiling the whole business. We therefore decided not to dress again until there was reason to expect a wagon to be going out at exactly the right time. We had smashed the lamps on the stairs on 11th, 12th, and 13th—the German was very keen on light and always replaced them—but for some reason which we never discovered he posted no sentry to watch them and took no apparent notice of the damage. He must have been playing some very deep game, but, since the lamp-smashing stopped after our departure and he could not connect us with it, it was never played out.

On the afternoon of 18th November a small party of British soldiers was told off to gather up the paper, straw, etc., from the room in which our parcels were unpacked and censored. They were to have it baled up and ready for loading on to a wagon at 5.30 p.m. This was just what we were waiting for. The oldest soldier was let into the conspiracy and asked to arrange for the loading to be completed at exactly 5.30—and he carried out his instructions almost to the second.

We had a big feed, with exactly the right quantity of German brandy, and were dressed and ready a few minutes before the hour.

On the stroke of the half-hour the wagon was signalled. We left our room and the building and walked down the yard towards the gate, accompanied by an English officer—dressed as a Russian to make the party look more commonplace—who was talking bad German to us at the top of his voice. We were very much encouraged by meeting some French and Russian officers, who, in all innocence, gave us the grudging salute on which the German always insisted. We carried in our hands the bunches of papers which seemed to be part of the dress of the German staff officer, and each smoked the customary foul cigar.

While the gate was being unlocked we stopped and exchanged the customary series of salutes and bows with our imitation Russian, and, that over, turned and walked out by the side of the wagon. The gate sentry jerked himself to attention, the Sergeant of the guard dropped his keys and saluted, and the worst was over. We politely returned the salutes and walked ahead of the wagon towards the gate in the outer fence. Here the sentry, whose job it was to unlock it, remained at ease, staring with open mouth at the two strange officers and apparently trying to screw himself up to draw their attention to the regulations by which no pedestrian might pass through his gate. Possibly he was expecting an order from us, but this was something we were quite unable to give him.

We were brought up short by the gate, and were both of us silently wondering what on earth to do next, the situation for a moment looking desperate, when, in despair, I raised a finger as if returning

THE ESCAPE CEREMONIAL

the salute which he had so far forgotten himself as to omit. He must have realised that he, a private soldier, was standing at ease within a yard of two officers—than which, in Prussia, it would be hard to imagine a more appalling situation. Seized with remorse he hurled himself at the gate, threw it open, clicked his heels and froze to attention. We walked out, acknowledged some jerks from the sentry on the fence and strolled down the road towards the town. We had to walk down some hundreds of yards of main road—Harrison going dead lame and rattling like a cheap-jack, a tin of biscuits having come adrift in his trousers—before we came to the turning down which we hoped to get into cover. I had made several visits, under escort, to a dentist, for the purpose of reconnoitring the surroundings of the camp, and knew of cover close by if we could only get into it unobserved. We were lucky, and within five minutes of leaving my room we were hidden between a couple of greenhouses in a large garden.

We hastily peeled off our caps, coats, leggings, etc., and stuffed them, with the rucksacks and food, into the sacks, put on civilian caps and emerged as heavily laden workmen.

Harrison wore a service-dress cap, deprived of its stuffing and dyed in ink. I wore one which had been given to a British soldier in a soldiers' camp. The playful Hun had decorated it with an identification patch of yellow paint, but this was easily removed.

It was only when we emerged from the garden that Harrison, who is a complete non-smoker, discovered that he had smoked his cigar right through and that it was singeing his moustache.

We passed the camp again at a little distance, and were rather disappointed not to see the fire-works which had been planned. I forget exactly what had occurred to spoil the show, but we were not unduly worried since, if there was no great conflagration, there was certainly no other sort of commotion, as there would surely be had any suggestion of an escape reached the sergeant of the guard.

'According to plan' we made our first night's march due east along a canal bank—the direction in which we least wanted to go but also the one in which the Germans were least likely to look for us. After going at top speed for five or six miles we stopped, got rid of most of the traces of our dis-guise, and removed the surplus clothing, which was only needed for the daily hide. The caps, Harrison's red collar, his shoulder-straps, patches, buttons and other frills were done up in my cape, which was weighted with stones and sunk in the canal. We had broken up and thrown away the swords at our first quick change.

After this we got on much more comfortably, with our baggage properly stowed in rucksacks. A good deal of rain and sleet was falling and we only met two or three men, with whom we exchanged the customary '*n'Abend*'—the only German to which we were prepared to commit ourselves. We roused a good many dogs on barges and in cottages, which alarmed us horribly at first, but we soon learnt that no one took any notice of them. We made detours round all the locks, hamlets and other places where more than a few solitary natives were likely to be met.

At the first streak of dawn we began to look for cover and were lucky in finding, without much searching, a large Dutch barn, full of straw and with no habitation near it. We climbed to the top of the straw, dug down between it and the end of the roof, put on all our extra clothing, and made ourselves as comfortable as we could. We had lost our water-bottle (a rubber air-cushion, with a funnel as filler) while collecting water from a ditch during the night, so had to carry up the day's supply in tins. We did this, of course, in the early morning before digging ourselves in. It was rather cold, but we spent a quiet day without any interruptions. During the day we got rid of the last traces of Prussian glory from Harrison's coat.

We allowed ourselves two hot drinks during the day, one of oxo and one of 'Bivouac' cocoa. The daily ration worked out at about eight ounces of chocolate, four small Plasmon biscuits and half a tin of potted meat each, and the two hot drinks. We had a lot of malted milk and beef tabloids which we sucked on the march. This unpleasant diet provided plenty of nourishment but precious little bulk, and we soon learnt the value of tight belts. We had reckoned on reaching the coast in fourteen nights but we did it in nine, so were able to increase our rations towards the end.

This first day was typical of the next nine. We always hid in barns, in spite of the rather greater risk of discovery, because we did not care to face the cold and damp of the woods with such a long walk before us. Only twice more were we lucky enough to find isolated barns; the other days we had to spend in villages, in barns which were close to their owners' homesteads and often communicated directly with the kitchen. The barns were mostly very big and contained large stacks of corn or straw. Dug well in to the top of a stack, at the end farthest from the ladder, we felt fairly safe. The farm people often came into the barns, and sometimes worked in them all day, but only once were we in real danger of discovery. This was when we were in a small barn and lying in hay instead of the more usual straw (it was much warmer) and a farm hand came up three times during the day to get food for the beasts. The first time we were not expecting him and he nearly walked right on to us, and came much too close with his pitchfork. After that we dug down about six feet into the hay, and he might have stood on us without spotting us.

Harrison used to sleep like a babe nearly all day and could hardly keep awake long enough to have his hot drinks. I felt the cold and could not sleep, except for the first hour after we got in, when I slept from sheer fatigue.

It began to snow a little on the sixth night of our walk and at the same time a very hard frost set in and held to the end of the trek. For the last day and night it snowed hard and continuously.

We generally marched from dusk, about 5.30 p.m., till the first signs of dawn at about 4.30 a.m. Sometimes our start was delayed by the farm people working later than usual and preventing our breaking out. One Sunday morning we stayed out until 5 a.m., thinking the natives would lie in bed a little longer than usual, but we were nearly caught out by the farmer, who came in just as we got to the top of our stack, and we had to lie doggo for an hour or more before he left us to dig in in peace.

We generally halted for an hour or an hour and a half, if we could find some sort of shelter, at about 11 p.m., but it was too cold for us to get much rest.

We drank, if possible, from ditches and ponds, but sometimes had to tackle a pump in the small hours of the morning. We were often chased away from one farm after another by barking dogs when in search of a good barn.

All the barns which we used had big double doors of thin match-boarding. To open them, I used to lie down on my back and pull one flap with my hands while I pushed the other with my feet. In this way I could bend the boards and make a gap through which Harrison could crawl; he then lit a candle, found the fastening bar and let me in.

During one lie-up Harrison crept down during the day, armed with a chocolate tin, to rob a cow which we thought we could hear moving about in a stall somewhere below us. He did a long and careful stalk, practically in darkness and found—a bull.

After the first night's march we went north-west, on a compass bearing across country, to hit off the Rostock road about thirty kilometres north of Burg. We had made up our minds not to pass through a single village until we had crossed the river Havel (about seventy kilometres north of Burg), and we made detours through the fields round every one. There was a village every three or four kilometres. There was, however, a light railway which circled round the outsides of the villages, and by following this we saved a good deal of time, though the going was far from good. We thought there might be some kind of organised look-out for us on the bridge at Havelberg, where our road crossed the river, so made for the bank some distance below the town in the hope of finding a boat. We found ourselves in a marsh cut up by innumerable channels, and, being unable to find any sort of boat, had to go back to the road. There was a strong light on the bridge, thrown from some kind of engine-house which stood at the far side of it, and we could see several people moving about. As we approached the road from the marsh we passed through some gardens in which was a large pile of faggots. We took some of the biggest of these on our heads and staggered wearily across the bridge, exchanging the usual greetings with one or two men of whom, on account of our loads, we could see nothing except the feet. We left the faggots in the first yard which we passed. Probably some one had to do time for stealing them.

The road was nearly straight most of the way and fairly easy to follow, the greatest difficulty being to hit off the right one when emerging from big villages and small towns. We never hesitated in towns, but always walked straight through and, if we came out on the wrong road, we never turned back but went across country until we struck the right one. This sometimes lost us an hour or more, since the country close to the towns was very much enclosed. In the open country the roads are always flanked on both sides by trees, and are therefore, easy to find even on a very dark night. We did not have to use the compass much—always a slow process at night—since, until the last three nights, the sky was fairly clear, and as long as we could see the pole-star ahead of us we knew that we could not be far out of the right direction.

We put into one sack everything which would not stow comfortably into our rucksacks and took it in turns to carry it for half-hour spells. We walked about four miles an hour.

Three nights from the finish I acquired a very warm blanket-lined coat, which was a great comfort.

Its owner, who had made a nuisance of himself by working in our barn all day, was thoughtful enough to leave it there when he knocked off for the German equivalent of tea just when it was time for us to be moving. When we were brought back to Burg the Commandant seized on this coat as conclusive evidence that we had been helped to escape by a German. (In civil life he was a judge.)

On the last night I had just got to the ground (we were in a very large Dutch barn) and Harrison was half-way down a very ramshackle staging when I saw two figures approaching through the snow with a huge covering of some sort over their heads. I whispered to Harrison, who kept as still as possible half-way down the scaffolding. I then dropped on my stomach at the foot of the staging. The two figures came into the barn, threw off the covering and disclosed themselves as young women. At the same moment Harrison's staging began to rattle violently, and the women, evidently in mortal terror, ran together and hugged each other. However, the rattling ceased and they began to peer about the barn, coming quite close to me and apparently looking straight at me, but seeing nothing. Then they picked up their covering, which turned out to be a huge mattress, and began hastily to fill it with unthreshed wheat from the stacks. Evidently they were robbing the barn and were just as anxious as we were not to be discovered, but it was not until some time afterwards that we realised this; at the moment we only felt sure we were spotted. I had another nerve-racking half-minute before they left us. The German peasant is nothing if not natural, and one of our visitors, having occasion to withdraw a little from her companion, chose—fortunately without examining it too closely—the very patch of darkness which was hiding me.

They went back to the road by the line which we had intended to follow, so, supposing that some habitation lay that way, we made off in the opposite direction—a change of plan for which we paid very heavily—meaning to circle round and get back to the road about a mile farther on.

For this last march we had no map, but we knew there was a choice of two roads, one running north-east through a place called Lage and the other north-west through Schwaan. We found neither place, nor did we get back to the main road until we were within two or three miles of Rostock. Between 6 p.m. on 26th November and 1.30 a.m. on 27th we covered about twenty-three miles, all either across country or on the worst of country roads—under a foot of snow. The result was that we arrived in Rostock completely tired out—a great mistake. In our later attempts we always planned to have a very short march on the last night so as to arrive at or near the frontier fresh and fit for any unforeseen emergency.

The going on those country lanes was very bad; they had been cut into deep ruts the mud of which was frozen as hard as stone and the snow was so deep that in the dark the surface appeared to be quite smooth. The consequence was that we trod on a ridge and twisted an ankle more or less at every step. It snowed hard almost the whole night and was so cold that we only tried once to rest, and gave it up after a few minutes. We found no water, every ditch, stream or pond being frozen hard (the thermometer marked $-20°$ centigrade, they told us afterwards in Rostock), and we were forced to quench our thirst by sucking handfuls of snow—anyone who has ever tried this will know that it causes the tongue to break into a mass of small blisters, a most painful condition.

We came into the outskirts of Rostock at about 1.30 a.m. and there made the acquaintance of a most amazingly stupid German sergeant-major.

We were following the main road towards the docks when he stepped out from the shadow of some trees and called on us to halt. We shuffled on a few paces, but he roared again, and, not having a run left in us, we could only adopt the tactics on which we had agreed for this sort of emergency and pretend to be slightly drunk. We halted and stood swaying slightly and looking stupidly at the German.

I think I have said that we spoke no German; to be more exact, I had a very, very thin smattering of the language, and Harrison had an even thinner one, but we could both understand the gist of anything likely to be said to us in such circumstances as these.

The German stood under a lamp and ordered one of us to advance. I staggered forward and he began to bellow at me: 'Who are you?' 'What are you?' 'Where do you come from?' 'Where are you going and why?' etc., etc. I looked drunkenly at him, but did not venture on an answer. He followed up with the inevitable: 'What nationality are you, and have you got papers?'—his voice getting louder and louder as he began to revel in the certainty of having found something really easy to bully. I began, between hiccoughs, to deliver a sentence in a mixture of languages which was meant to explain that we were Danish sailors from a ship in the docks, that we did not speak German, that we had left our papers in the ship, that we had been drinking with friends at the canal docks (we had just passed them and heard sounds of carousal), that German beer was very good and we were only poor sailors, and he was a dear good, kind Prussian officer of very high rank and it was very cold. Good-night!

He seemed to follow my meaning, for he kept repeating my words, with corrections, at the top of his voice.

He tore open my coat and examined my clothes, finally running his finger down the seam of my trousers to feel for a stripe—which was there! Then he pushed me back against a wall and called up Harrison, who, during this performance, had been giving a wonderfully realistic imitation of a drunken man being sick in the gutter. Harrison let him roar half a dozen times, each roar angrier than the last, then staggered towards him, and, when he was right up against him, let go, with appropriate music, a full mouthful of chewed snow and chocolate all over the hero's manly breast. He was wearing a brand-new great-coat of the expensive pale blue kind which German under-officers are allowed to have made at their own expense. He screamed with rage, and, hurling Harrison violently away from him, treated us for three minutes to the choicest flow of obscenities to which he could lay his tongue while he scraped his chest with a piece of stick.

Then, to our utter amazement, he said something about having thought at first that we were prisoners of war and we could (not very politely) get out of his sight for a couple of blank, blank foreigners.

From start to finish we neither of us thought for a moment that we had the slightest chance of bluffing that Hun—or any other—and had always agreed that, once fairly suspected, our only hope lay in running. Had our friend thought of looking in our packs he could not have failed to realise what we were. We learnt later at the police station that he was on the look-out for a couple of Russian privates who had bolted from a working party at Stralsund, but he actually knew that two British officers were reported escaped and that the Magdeburg Command had offered two hundred marks for the recapture of either.

After this incident we continued to walk drunkenly whenever there was anyone in sight. We often found the drunken walk useful during later attempts.

We made straight for the docks, and soon found a road which ran their whole length and quite close to the water-side. We had originally intended to have only a preliminary look at the docks that night, and, unless we hit on the ferry-steamer at once and it seemed fairly easy to board, to push right on to the open coast and try for something in the way of a small boat the next night. But our cross-country trek had taken so much out of us that we decided to try there and then to get on board some kind of neutral steamer. We walked the whole length of the docks, meeting only one policeman, who was not interested in us, and seeing a great many steamers, several of which appeared to be neutrals.

It was an ideal night for our purpose, snowing and freezing hard, with a biting wind, and we knew quite well that any watchmen who might be posted about the docks would be in their huts with the doors closed and braziers going full blast. We moved without a sound over the snow. The docks were fairly well lit.

Eventually we hit on a small steamer lying alongside the quay, with a little smoke coming from her funnel. She had the Danish flag painted on her side and an obviously Scandinavian name under her counter. We looked her over from end to end, saw that there was no sign of a watch on deck and were on the point of creeping up her gangway when a big German police-dog rushed up from behind and jumped around us, barking noisily.

The door of a shed opened and a policeman walked up to us holding a whistle to his mouth. We tried the drunkard business, but we were up against a man of very different type to our sergeant-major friend. We were on enclosed premises, and in any case we could not run, so that was the end of our first attempt.

We were taken to the police station, where we shared the remains of our condensed rations with the police, who, for a small consideration, agreed to forget all about them. Consequently, when we were searched at Burg nothing was found to show how we had lived, and the Germans flatly refused to believe that we had walked from Burg or fed from our pockets. Moreover, no suspicion fell at that time on the concentrated foods which continued to arrive in every parcel from home.

The police treated us very civilly. We spent the rest of the night together in a rather lousy cell, and, after a hearty breakfast of mangold soup next morning, were ordered to prepare for the journey back to Burg. This instruction was given to us by a handcuffed prisoner, who was produced to act as interpreter. He told us incidentally that he was a Swedish sailor and that he had been condemned to death the day before on charges of espionage.

We were taken over at the police station by an

escort consisting of two of the most ferocious-looking sergeants I ever set eyes on—enormous men with fat, pink necks, bulging pink eyes and ginger moustaches on the model of the All Highest. They came to our cell, after we had been told to dress for

A STROLL THROUGH ROSTOCK

the journey, and peremptorily ordered us out of it. Then each produced a firearm—one a revolver, the other an automatic pistol—which they ostentatiously loaded, cocked and waved in our faces with the customary blood-curdling threats.

I mention this not because it was unusual but because of what followed in the train.

By the time we reached the station we had them half tamed, and they allowed us to buy—for all four of us—the most substantial meal which the refreshment-room could produce. We had to finish it on the platform because the head waiter unfortunately discovered that we were English pig-dogs and not poor deserters and kicked us out of the room. He got no tip. When we were in the train, however, our escort received some whispered instructions from the local equivalent of a railway transport officer, which brought on a fresh spasm of ferocity, and the pistols were again produced and their moving parts exercised for our benefit.

The result was that the automatic jammed at half-cock, with a cartridge half in the chamber and the muzzle within six inches of my stomach; but when I put out my hand for it and suggested to its owner in pidgin-German that he had better let me have it since I understood its works and he did not, he handed it over like a lamb, and only breathed freely again when I had removed the magazine and extracted the jammed cartridge. I told him it was a very dangerous instrument, and he thankfully followed my advice to put it in one pocket and the cartridges in the other and keep them as far as possible apart until he had had some more lessons in their use. In the next three years I learnt that these were quite a common type of home-serving

German, but at the time we were both a little surprised.

We arrived at Magdeburg at 10 p.m. and Hauptmann Chessmann, the Burg Commandant, was so overjoyed at the thought of seeing us again after mourning us as lost for ever (and probably having been severely 'strafed') that he came in person to meet us and held a preliminary inquiry on the spot while we waited for our connection.

We were rather roughly handled by the guard which took us on from Magdeburg to Burg—probably they had had a pretty thin time in consequence of our escape.

I should mention here that, when we were preparing to quit the camp, we wanted to make the Germans think, if we succeeded in getting out, that we had gone by train to Holland so that the look-out in the other directions might be less strict. Harrison therefore wrote a note which he addressed to an English officer, Templer, who was doing time for some trivial offence in Burg prison. In the note (which he mentioned would be smuggled into prison by a corrupted German) he said: 'If we are not with you by the day after to-morrow we shall be in Holland. The Germans do not know that Cartwright speaks German so will never dream that we are going by train.' He left the note among his belongings, where it was found as soon as we were missed. The Commandant swallowed it whole. It was dramatically produced at the official inquiry to prove me a liar when I denied that I knew the language. When I left Germany the following entry still stood in my 'conduct sheet': 'Speaks German perfectly, but will not admit it.' This has been brought up at every court martial or court of inquiry at which I have had the pleasure of assisting since that date.

At the inquiry after our recapture a pair of English gloves and a tin-opener were produced as evidence against us. They were supposed to support a trumped-up charge of burglary. The things had been found in the garden where we did our first quick change—which, by a curious coincidence, happened to be the Commandant's own garden—and a broken board in the fence was the basis of the burglary charge. Harrison said he wanted the post office parcels register produced as evidence for us. Asked by the Commandant what he meant, he replied: 'To prove that enough prisoners' parcels have arrived at the post office, and have not been signed for by the addressees, to outfit the whole population of Burg with English goods.' We heard no more of the burglary charge.

The glove question was the only one which we answered at all, so that, since the Germans had not the slightest idea how we really got out, the inquiry was not a success. In subsequent interrogations and inquiries of the same kind we have both always declined to answer a single question. This makes the German very angry, since, failing evidence, he always charges a prisoner on 'his own confession' if he has opened his mouth at all. Even if he has not he gets no peace until he has signed a long statement, in German, alleged to be a verbatim report of the inquiry. I always willingly signed these novels, writing over my signature : 'I do not understand the above.' This too seemed to make them angry.

After we had left the camp the officers in our room—all British—had tried to fake the 9 p.m. roll-call for us, so as to give us a longer start. The evening roll-call was a hasty run round the rooms by an officer and two or three underlings. They made dummies to represent us nd stood them in the darkest corners of the rooms. Unfortunately the man whose job it was to stand so as almost to obscure the view of the first dummy stood a little too close to it, with the result that, just as the German officer turned to leave the room, some movement caused the dummy to fall and its head rolled out at his feet. The subsequent proceedings were rather sultry and very Prussian.

One English officer had flatly refused to have anything to do with the dummy-making or to allow any of his property to be used. When we arrived at my old home, the Burg jail, where we were taken straight from the train on arrival from Rostock, this old friend was the first person to greet us. He was doing ten days for complicity in our escape. The German does occasionally do the right thing !

It is perhaps worth mentioning some of the

difficulties under which we prepared for this and subsequent attempts. I have already given some of the reasons which made secrecy, even from Englishmen and allies, so necessary. At this time (1915) there had been only one successful escape, and that by a man who spoke perfect German and was interned only fifteen miles from the Dutch frontier. A certain very small number of British officers therefore adopted an attitude of lofty contempt for those who, they said, were 'trying to earn notoriety at the expense of the comfort of the general community.' Four officers in particular were known to the scoffers in one camp as the 'escape maniacs,' and every obstacle known to the passive resister was placed in their way. Eventually the maniacs all escaped. One of them was killed in France, two went back to active service there, and were twice promoted, while the fourth only succeeded in reaching Boulogne on the day of the Armistice. The scoffers had nearly all been captured in the very early days of the war, and most of them probably honestly believed that escape was impossible and that their view was the official one at home. The War Office later gave material evidence that it did not agree. At their worst they were a very small minority, but they did manage to make things appreciably more difficult.

There had been quite a number of utterly useless but more or less spectacular attempts to break out by men who had made no preparations and could not possibly hope to succeed even if they managed to get out of their camps. The scoffers judged all attempts by these. Actually the notoriety-hunters were execrated far more by those prisoners who really meant to get away than by the scoffers, for the net result of each and every one of their efforts was to close a possible hole. The perpetrators were mostly—but not quite all—Russians.

While the attitude of the scoffers made our preparations no easier, the fact that the Germans might at any moment descend in mass and search the whole or any part of a camp made them very much more difficult. They would suddenly surround one or more buildings with sentries and systematically search every room, finally stripping the occupants naked and searching their clothing. At Burg the soldiers who conducted the searches sometimes had the help of two or three dozen Magdeburg detectives—if they were a fair sample the Magdeburg criminal should lead a care-free life. One of these searches took place soon after Harrison and I had begun our preparations and when our uniforms were more than half made; every stitch of our clothing was examined, but nothing suspicious was noticed except the half-made swords. The officer to whom these were triumphantly brought by the finder remarked that he saw no harm in the English amateurs playing at soldiers if it amused them.

We were five weeks in the civil prison but since, in spite of continual interrogations, we refused to convict ourselves, and the Germans had no evidence at all and could not think out any which would fit the facts, we were never brought to trial. In the last week some one in the camp did describe to the Germans exactly how we had escaped, and the assistant Commandant (known to his flock as Rumblebelly, but he probably had another name) had the whole story beautifully typed out in English for us to sign. Of course we refused, and when we pointed to our various articles of clothing—in particular my beautiful yellow boots, which I had converted into shoes—he had to admit that the story was an impossible one. The informer, whoever he was, probably had a rough passage for putting up such a ridiculous yarn. They had previously put up three or four other accounts for our approval, all of which, they had said in turn, could be proved by overwhelming evidence. They do not know to this day how we got out.

On the 29th of December 1915 the Commandant and Rumblebelly came to our cells and informed us that we need not waste time on any further plans, since we were to be separated and would not meet again in Germany. The same day Harrison was sent to Torgau and I to Halle.

I hinted above that the Germans were not always very clever searchers but perhaps it is only fair to say that a crowd of British officers, herded together in a very small space, was not the easiest thing to search. For one thing, they simply would not stay put, but insisted on circulating in spite of every kind of abuse and the oft-repeated and sometimes executed threat of instant arrest. Thus I have seen a really keen officer searched three times in the course of a single visit while a more retiring and bashful brother-officer was not searched at all—but the number of *Herren* searched apparently tallied with the number of beds in the room, so what could be wrong? Again, they were apt to be insistent, not to say officious, in their efforts to help the searchers in their disagreeable and difficult job. For instance, when a German had made a heap, on the table perhaps, of properties from one corner of the room and was about to go through them, an over-zealous British helper would add twice the volume of already searched properties from another corner—and vice versa—and in the ensuing dash to separate the two lots quite possibly the whole bunch, and the table, would collapse on the floor. It was all very difficult and confusing for the German, who was really doing his best, and sometimes he got quite irritable.

Then the German is a shocking bad counter, and he cannot live without lists and the checking of lists, and the lists are hardly ever quite right. At Küstrin once he searched a room and at the first dart unearthed a forbidden felt hat. One of his assistants placed the hat on a table while another licked his pencil and wrote: '*Ein Hut*' in a notebook. The search continued. Presently the hat vanished from the table, unnoticed by the searchers, but the same one was discovered soon afterwards stuffed into some one's mattress, whence it was dragged in triumph and again placed on the table with the rest of the bag. (We always provided a lot of useless but forbidden trash, hidden in the most obvious places; this prevented the searchers from becoming despondent and gave the tally-clerk a job to keep him quiet.) Again '*Ein Hut*' was written in the note-book and the work proceeded. Again the hat, unnoticed, vanished from the table and again it was found, this time hanging by a string outside the window. For the third time '*Ein Hut*' was written in the book, and still the good work went on. Finally, when all was over, the bag was laid out to be checked and each article was ticked off by the tally-clerk as it was dropped into a basket for removal. There remained three items unticked in the note-book, each of them reading '*Ein Hut*,' and this by simple addition makes '*Drei Hute*,' but not a single hat could be found in the bag.

One can imagine what would have happened had this game been tried by German prisoners in an English camp, but it was just the sort of situation with which the German—at all events the second-rate kind which was found in and about prison camps—could not compete. They pretended there was nothing wrong, withdrew noisily and left that room severely alone in the next search.

III
TORGAU

By M. C. C. HARRISON

Collecting of stores—Secret information in parcels—Methods of escape—Walks on parole—Campbell's tunnel—Mobilisation kit—Escape with Lesaffres through the tunnel—Walking to the Baltic—Recapture on the coast—Return via Berlin to Torgau—Planning escape from Torgau civil prison—A court martial—Removal to Magdeburg.

WHEN the 29th December 1915 arrived I was very pleased to find myself once more in Torgau. There were few changes since I had left the place in June. The English colony had increased to ten, and were fortunate in having amongst their number Lieut. and Quartermaster Hammond, Royal Marine Light Infantry, who undertook the responsibility of checking all our parcels with German officers in a room on the ground floor of the main building. His masterful manner over these individuals caused them to be afraid of interfering beyond seeing each tin opened. He would never let them tamper with the contents of a seven-pound biscuit-tin once they had seen the top row.

This would give an opportunity of collecting maps, compasses, wire-cutters, etc., etc., if only the information could be conveyed home.

There were now about four hundred and fifty French, four hundred and fifty Russians and twenty Belgians in the camp, but all had been made far more comfortable. Prisoners had been allowed to erect partitions between their beds with wood procured through the commandant's office.

The administrative work was now entirely carried out by a large staff of Germans. Recreation within the camp was also well organised, and, taking all things into consideration, conditions were fairly satisfactory.

I might here mention that as the summer of 1915 had passed without appreciably altering the positions on the Western Front, the war looked as if it was going to last for ever from the prisoner's point of view, and hence the determined fight by a large number for better conditions. The majority of the French, captured at Maubeuge, belonged to reserve regiments, and a large number of these officers had occupied themselves in improving their skill at their own trade or devoting their time to some particular hobby such as work on huckaback or manufacture of wooden clocks.

Early in 1916 pressure from an influential source resulted in the French who had been in captivity for over a year being allowed to send home parcels containing work they had completed as prisoners. Each French officer would bring his work, when ready for dispatch, to the parcel room, where an under-officer would examine it before repacking and sealing it up for dispatch. As time continued slackness developed, and if the under-officer was particularly busy, as was generally the case just before the morning roll-call, he would tell the officer to tie up his own parcel, while he himself did something else.

Now one of the most valuable lessons I had learnt from my recent experiences was the importance of absolute secrecy. To breathe one word, or even to arouse suspicion unnecessarily, was to court disaster. Camps were full of spies, mostly disguised as allied orderlies, but in reality employed for no purpose other than to pick up conversations connected with escapes. I had witnessed so many disasters at Burg, brought about by spies overhearing young officers idly discussing the possibilities of some one's contemplated escape, that I suppose I was unnecessarily guarded in this respect. My policy was to let every one in the camp think I hadn't the least intention of trying to escape again, and to support this I used to take part in most of the silly games.

I carefully selected a young French officer, Lieut. Lesaffres, to teach me his language in exchange for English lessons. Swearing him to secrecy I confided to him alone that I hadn't the least intention of stopping in the camp longer than absolutely necessary. I told him of the importance of collecting certain mobilisation stores before making any attempt, and promised to bring him with me if he would smuggle a message home in a parcel. I had chosen my man well and he agreed at once.

At the time, I had not definitely made up my mind what was the best way out of the camp, though I very much favoured going out as German officers again. The authorities at Burg, after converting my guard's coat into a military garment, had returned it to me more like a German officer's coat than ever, and there were plenty of Russian capes and French red trousers to be had. We were, however, obliged to wait for two or three months before we could hope to receive any of the articles I was now writing home for.

Lessaffres prepared a large parcel containing, amongst other articles, a cylindrical tin about the size of a two pound pot of jam. We made a false bottom to this and I wrote home on circular bits of paper a long list of my requirements, with instructions as to how each should be sent. In addition to maps, compasses, metal saws and files, wire-cutters, electric lamps, brandy, concentrated food and solid methylated spirit, I also asked for arrangements to be made with some Danish traders to have a boat lying alongside at any quiet place on the Baltic between certain hours on selected days, and, as a further precaution, I asked for any information that could be furnished about the Dutch frontier.

Torgau was about two hundred and fifty miles from the Baltic and three hundred and fifty miles from Holland, but I did not anticipate much difficulty in getting to either place.

It might be interesting here to divide an escape into three phases and observe the relative difficulties as they appeared to the prisoner:

1. Getting out of the camp.
2. The walk through Germany.
3. Crossing the frontier.

In the early stages of the war (1) was comparatively easy, (2) an unknown quantity and for a time an apparent impossibility, and (3) also unknown but not quite as difficult as (2).

At the time of smuggling this letter home (2) was undoubtedly the easiest; (1) had become much harder; and (3) was looked on as the most difficult. I therefore decided to try and get all the outside assistance I could to compete with (3).

Lesaffres had to take on the job of bluffing the under-officer in the parcel room, and, choosing his time well, he experienced no difficulty; and as our plans developed indents for further supplies were smuggled home. Lesaffres became so proficient at bluffing the censor that he even succeeded in smuggling my autograph book, which contained pictures done at both Burg and Torgau by artists of all the allies. Keeping this inside his coat till the under-officer had examined the contents of his parcel he slipped it in at the last moment. The plans which appear in these pages are from this book.

Realising that the Germans must soon tumble to the fact that prisoners were able to send home secret information by these parcels, it was obvious

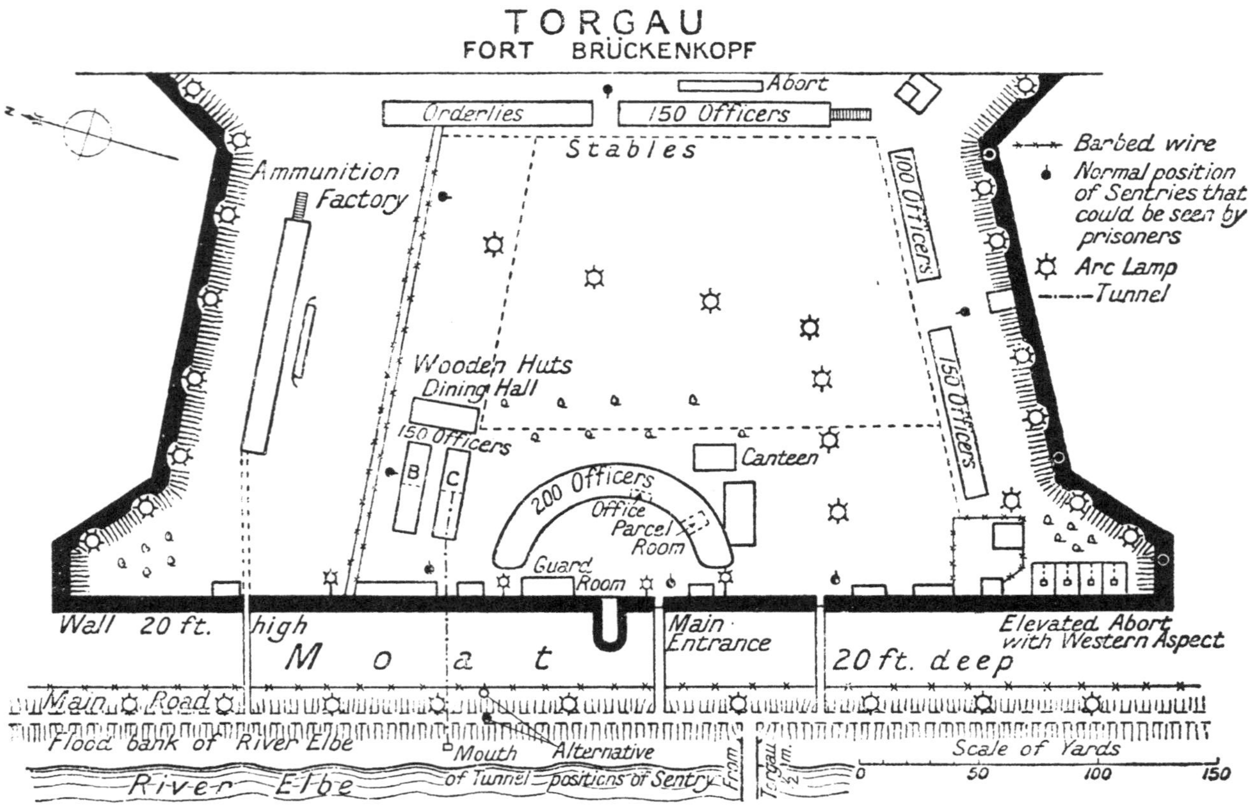

TORGAU
FORT BRÜCKENKOPF

PLAN OF TORGAU

that the privilege would soon be removed. I therefore asked for invisible ink, with all instructions, to be sent to me. Each tin containing contraband in a parcel sent to me was to be labelled 'Love from Frances,' so that I could be fully prepared.

Little remained to be done now but to decide on the method of getting out of the camp. Strange German officers did not visit the camp as often as they did at Burg. In vain I searched for a place to scale the walls. To get into the munition factory enclosure (see plan) and then do so appeared a possibility. The officers' cell at the military prison on the other side of the Elbe looked very promising. I had been in this cell during my previous stay at Torgau. It was more like a room than a cell, and had two windows with comparatively thin bars. It was situated on the first floor overlooking a small garden surrounded by a wall not more than seven feet high. The guards visited the cell every two hours during the night and tested the bars, but this being a matter of routine, would hardly have been a sufficient precaution to interfere with a determined attempt. As there was only one officers' cell the trouble was how were two of us going to manage ?

I decided to go to prison again to make a further reconnaissance. I did not notice the Commandant when I passed him next morning, and was given three days' imprisonment. Some officer from the other camp in Torgau was occupying the officers' cell, so I was put into one of the smaller ones. This was extremely fortunate as it gave me an opportunity of examining the inside of these smaller cells which one of us, at any rate, must occupy if we both went to prison at the same time.

The bars were thicker and more inaccessible than

I DID NOT NOTICE THE COMMANDANT

those in the officers' cell, but they were never examined and there was no interference at night.

At this time I was not an expert at picking locks, nor had I considered the possibility of making my own keys.

I got on the best possible terms I could with the jailer, and came away thoroughly satisfied with my investigations, as I had definitely discovered a workable means of escape, provided we could get into that prison properly mobilised. All that remained to be done now was to see if a better means of escape could be found out of the camp direct.

Soon after I came back from prison, officers who gave their parole that they would not try to escape were taken, *en masse*, with a weak guard, for walks in the country. When the notification was first given out, there was a most decided division in the camp. A strong portion firmly declined to have anything whatever to do with it, holding out that prisoners had no right to give their parole at any time, as this, if practised on a large scale, would enable the Germans to reduce their guards and produce more men for the Front. The Russians, *en masse*, firmly declined to have anything to do with it, but about eighty French officers and a few English decided to take this opportunity to get outside the four walls of the fortress.

Before exercise the party was paraded and checked on the open space in front of the guard-room, and the officer in charge took a card from each prisoner with a signed statement that he would not try to escape. All this was done thoroughly, and a German officer then led the way through the gate and the under-officers, engaged in checking, fell out. The party followed the officer and went for a walk in the country, frequently through woods. The authorities took every conceivable precaution to see that no one was on this parade who had not given in his parole card, but the sentry on the gate had no means of checking them as they went out. Adequate precautions were not taken to keep the remaining prisoners from crowding round the gate, and nothing appeared easier than to cause a slight diversion for the sentry and pass out at the same time, disguised as French officers.

I give this account in detail as it is liable to criticism. I stand by the decision I made to go out this way, as it was most certainly up to the Germans to see that no officer passed through the gate, other than those who had given their parole.

The camp was soon well acquainted with full particulars of the routes followed on these walks. We were only waiting for my mobilisation stores, and neither of us breathed a word of our intention to anyone until May, when Captain MacAllan, Cameronians, was about to be invalided to Switzerland. He lived in my room and shared the same mess in the dining-hall. I told him I hoped to go in about a month's time, and as I expected to be another month in the country, I asked him when he got to Switzerland to write and tell my people not to worry if they did not get any letters from me for a long period.

Lieut. Colin Campbell, Argyll and Sutherland Highlanders, also shared the same mess (just four or five English Officers), and, curiously enough, he also confided similar information to MacAllan. The latter seeing that the two escapes were about to take place at the same time, and fearing that one might interfere with the other, dropped a hint to each of us about the other.

Colin Campbell lived in the Hut C. I call it C because he appeared to have made himself so comfortable in the corner of one of the rooms by neatly partitioning off his bed that it was known as 'Château Campbell.' He shared the room with about fifteen French and fifteen Russian officers, and seemed to spend most of his time studying Russian with some officers who lived in a room at the other end of the camp. These Russians in turn would come to him to learn English. Such was the occupation of many prisoners of war. I liked Campbell very much, but not for one moment did I ever dream that he could contemplate an escape, as I knew how badly he had been wounded.

Trading on the principle that it is inadvisable to discuss a proposed escape with anyone beyond the absolute minimum necessary for its execution, I had even gone out of my way to put him off the scent.

He told me now that he and three Russians had started a tunnel about the 15th December 1915, nearly five months previously, from underneath his bed. They had bored their way successfully underneath the moat, and were by now under the road beyond. They had had great difficulty with water, and all work had had to be suspended whenever the level of the Elbe had risen. The floor of his hut was about twelve inches off the ground, which afforded ample space for storing the excavated earth. As the tunnel increased in length they had roped in a few more workers, all Russians. For tools they had used their hands and fire-irons, while the earth was carried back in sandbags made of old clothes. Every inch had to be boarded, and the wood was provided partly from parcels and partly by the Russians, who lived in the other side of the camp. They had partitioned their beds off in twos and threes instead of singly so as to have surplus wood. Ventilation holes were bored into the moat and the work was carried out entirely by candle-light.

The whole scheme had been engineered by Campbell, and he told me he had thrown out many feelers to try and ascertain if I would join in it, and had come to the conclusion that I was definitely 'off' escaping. If it was important for me not to discuss my plans with outsiders, it was ten times more so for him. The magnitude of the work would have set the whole camp talking, and news would soon have reached the Germans. So carefully had he chosen his friends and kept his secret that my suspicions had been in no way aroused, although we had met every day at meals. The thoroughness paid to all detail can be gauged from the fact that although the tunnel actually started underneath his bed, not one of the remaining thirty officers of the room knew anything about it. That he was able to keep them in total darkness for over eight months is almost inconceivable, especially when it is realised that every one in a prisoners' camp who has no occupation of his own becomes extremely inquisitive about other people's affairs.

All wood for revetting was prepared in the Russians' room at the other end of the camp, and carried over to Campbell's in pieces inside overcoats after dusk.

The rate of work varied from one yard to half a yard a day according to the length of carry of the excavated earth.

I need hardly say how pleased I was to be enrolled as a working member. Although Lesaffres would eventually come with me through the tunnel, the Russians were firm that neither he nor any French officer was to be told about it till the last moment, as spies disguised as French orderlies had already been located in the camp.

My first glimpse of the tunnel filled me with admiration for all who had been secretly working at it for months, and particularly for Campbell who was responsible for all the engineering work.

I have already said the floor-boards of this hut were a foot above the ground. When the trap-door under Campbell's bed was removed to admit me I stepped straight into a trench three feet deep. I walked along the trench to the end of the building before entering the mouth of the tunnel, which descended at a slope of one over eight until the fortress wall was reached. The foundations of this wall were lower than had been expected, and I learned that great engineering difficulties arose in getting under it. To get the extra depth steps had now to be put into the tunnel. Water at this point was a serious menace, for not only had all work to be suspended directly there was the slightest rise in the level of the Elbe, but grave fears were entertained over the safety of removing the necessary amount of earth from the vicinity of the foundations of the wall.

The trench under the hut was extended in various directions so as to facilitate access to reception places for excavated earth, and also to furnish an underground changing-room where special old tunnelling clothes were kept.

It was possible to walk up to the wall in a crouching position, but to proceed the floor of the tunnel was kept only two feet below the foundations in order to avoid going to unnecessary depth. Directly this obstacle had been passed the tunnel was raised until the top was only two feet from the bottom of the moat, into which air-holes were pierced. This enabled work to be carried on here even when the portion below the wall was under water. The width now was one foot nine inches and the height two feet three inches, which is just sufficient to enable a man to crawl on hands and knees. To facilitate work, every ten or fifteen yards shunting places were provided by scooping away sufficient earth on one side to enable a man to lie down while another crawled by. On passing the moat the level was gradually raised, and as ventilation holes were no longer possible the air became so foul that candles would not remain alight. Direction, which could previously be checked by keeping candles in a line at intervals along the tunnel, could now only be maintained by luminous compass. By June there were fifteen workers, all Russians and English, and as Campbell was the only one who lived in this hut all work had to be carried out in the daytime. The following routine was observed :

We divided ourselves into three working-parties, each of five. Each party worked for two hours, when an interval of three hours was necessary to give the foul air at the end a chance of becoming more breathable. The procedure was that No. 1 at the end would burrow alone, filling sandbags as he progressed ; No. 2 would keep quite twenty yards behind No. 1, so as not to use any of his air, and would crawl up at intervals to drag a full sandbag back to his place ; No. 3 would be waiting ten or fifteen yards behind No. 2 ; and so on. Each would bring forward an empty sandbag as he crawled to collect a full one.

Twenty minutes was about as long as anyone could continue doing the work of No. 1.

When reliefs were working some one was always on duty in Campbell's room. This of course was generally Campbell himself, when he was not below. Before returning to the room from work special care was taken to wash and tidy up in the underground changing-room.

One day, before I had heard about the tunnel, Mr. Jackson of the American Embassy visited Torgau and all English prisoners were suddenly summoned to the Commandant's office. That Campbell could not be found immediately did not cause any undue alarm, as it was well known that he had many Russian friends and might be studying the language with any of them. A hasty search in all likely places failed to find him, and just as his prolonged absence was beginning to cause surprise he suddenly appeared. I forget where he said he had been, but he was actually doing the duty of No. 1. The Russian on duty in his room (apparently waiting for an English lesson) got the message to him, but it was some time before he could appear properly dressed and clean. My own suspicions were not aroused in any way, nor do I believe were anybody else's ; but I can well imagine his feelings as he arrived long after everybody else and was put through a series of questions by Mr. Jackson in the presence of the commandant and his staff, when in the midst of it all he suddenly felt some earth in his ear and wondered how much more mud he had failed to remove.

In June my mobilisation stores started to arrive. Most of them were in large tins of biscuits and, thanks to the skilful packing at home and the dictatorial manner of Hammond to the Germans in the parcel room, everything I asked for arrived safely. I suppose I must now have been in possession of about the finest mobilisation kit that any prisoner ever possessed, and I was glad to be able to help some of the original members of the tunnel in this respect.

My electric torches were very useful in the tunnel. Automobile maps to the Baltic and Holland were also a great asset. Unfortunately it had not been possible to arrange for facilities to be given to me to stow away on a Danish boat, and I was told no assistance could be rendered in this respect. I was disappointed as I believed it could have been arranged. I was, however, shown the exact position of two neighbouring sentries on the Dutch frontier.

My invisible ink, prepared by a well-known doctor in Ireland, was sent quite openly as medicine, and was duly delivered to me. It was subsequently of the greatest use, and in view of the label on it I never had to take any trouble to conceal the bottle during searches.

For a long cross-country walk it seemed advisable to carry brandy, and this I had asked to be sent in a bottle labelled 'Hair-wash.' The trick was, however, played out by the time mine arrived and, in spite of Hammond's protestations, the censor poured a little of the liquid on the table and lit it. He knew quite well it was brandy, as several officers had recently been caught doing the same thing. Hammond accounted for its lighting by the fact that English hair-wash was good and contained a certain amount of spirit, but the censor was firm and insisted on its going to the doctor to be analysed before letting me have it.

As the doctor had already left the camp, the bottle was locked up in the parcel room till the next day.

I have already said that I was not yet an expert at picking locks, so we burgled the room via the window that night, removed the brandy from the bottle and replaced it with some cheap German hair-wash. This was in due course analysed and returned to me with an apology, as some had been wasted in so doing. Hammond then told off the parcel under-officer like a pickpocket, with the result that he hardly dared interfere with any of our parcels in future.

Now that my mobilisation stores had arrived I had to decide what route I would follow. The others were all splitting up into parties of two or three, and, Torgau being so central, some were going to Switzerland, some Rumania, some Poland and some Denmark, but none to Holland.

We all expected the Dutch frontier would be better guarded than any other. Stories of live electric wire about a foot off the ground, near this frontier had been current in both Burg and Torgau.

I accordingly decided to go to the Baltic and try to steal a small boat.

The distance across the Baltic was only twenty miles ; from the ' Riddle of the Sands ' I knew there were no currents, and I was quite convinced that two of us could row across in a night if we failed to find a small sailing-boat. The distance to Holland was rather more than three hundred miles, over many rivers, whereas the Baltic was only two hundred and fifty miles, and I was already familiar with most of the road. As my objective I chose first Graal then Muritz, shown as bathing-places on my map. They were about three miles apart, and if we failed to find a suitable craft on that bit of coast we could try a fishing centre about eight miles farther east.

By the middle of June the tunnel was nearly ninety yards long, and it was becoming most important for us to ascertain our exact position. Though we could measure the length of the tunnel, without instruments we could only guess the distance from the Fort to the road, beyond which the ground sloped down gradually to the Elbe.

It was our intention to continue the tunnel for at least ten yards beyond the road before coming to the surface. The air had become so bad that it was doubtful whether we could continue without coming sufficiently close to the surface to bore for ventilation—a dangerous experiment at any time, but particularly so, near the road.

In order to find out the exact distance from the Fort to the farther side of the road, I gave the authorities an opportunity of sending me off to prison, which was easily done by being a little late for roll-call. As the journey to prison took me on to the main road, I was thus able to pace the exact distance from the fort to the farther side of the road.

By the end of July we had gone a hundred yards, when we managed to bore through about three feet of earth for air. Oh, what a relief!

I might here mention that in addition to the fifteen workers there was one Russian colonel to whom daily progress was reported. It was on his advice that a Russian engineer officer was now called in to assist in the difficult task of coming to the surface. We continued for another five feet, getting slightly closer to the surface. After a hundred and one yards two feet we decided to come up. The tunnel was widened at this point, and a chamber made sufficiently large to take a board two feet six inches by three feet. The board formed the roof at the end of the tunnel.

Every day from now on the earth above the board was scraped away and the board pushed higher up until only three inches of earth remained above it. When we were ready the first person to go out, Colin Campbell, could cut the earth round the edge of the board with a knife, place the board and sod in the specially-prepared chamber beyond the end of the tunnel, and the engineer officer, who was not coming with us, could replace it.

As the mouth of the tunnel would be brilliantly lit up by arc lights from the camp and could be readily seen from the road, this precaution seemed advisable. Campbell could get out of the tunnel without unnecessarily exposing himself, and the Russian who replaced the sod would incur the minimum amount of risk.

In August, shortly before completion, one of the Russians elected to have nothing more to do with the tunnel. He had done excellent work in it, doing, if anything, rather more than his share of No. 1. His attitude now was incomprehensible, and he soon dissociated himself from all our other Russians.

The next shock we received was when Lesaffres came and told me that he had heard all about the tunnel from this Russian, and that I was in it. He feared, at first, that I was about to let him down and escape with some one else, so I hastily assured him that we were to go together that way instead of adhering to our original plan, but that I had been sworn to secrecy and could not tell him anything till all was ready. The remainder were very concerned when they heard news had leaked out to the French. As I was actually going out with a French officer, I was afraid I would be looked on as the traitor, but the Russian colonel was quite satisfied that the information had leaked out through the Russian who had 'cried off.'

Everything was done to stop the news spreading, but it was too late. Nevertheless we kept it in check with counter-rumours.

With the help of spies in the camp the news soon reached the Germans. They even knew by name a large number of those engaged in the work, and as my name had been mentioned to Lesaffres I was one of the suspects. The Russians who had cut up the wood in the opposite side of the camp were also under suspicion, and it was in this area that the Germans concentrated their attention. Extra sentries were furnished at night, and the camp permanent staff could be seen prowling around there every evening.

We all brought our mobilisation stores into our underground changing-room and had everything ready there, so that when the time came we would only have to go into Campbell's room in ordinary uniform. Those who were under suspicion purposely spent most of the evenings at the far end of the camp, letting themselves be seen there as much as possible by the Germans employed specially to report on their movements.

I have already referred to the spies employed by the authorities against us and I might here add that the prisoners were seldom short of information concerning anything that went on in the camp Commandant's office. His own clerks sometimes resented the Prussian discipline and always welcomed any appetising food they could get from prisoners.

By the 14th August the tunnel was absolutely complete and the exit beautifully prepared. We could actually have gone out a night or two sooner if we had elected not to wait for so perfect a job to be made of the exit.

Now that the Germans were in possession of so much information, we were very concerned that they might find out too much before we could escape. To make a complete success we were more or less tied down to wait for an east wind, when the sentry on the road outside usually came into the moat for shelter. We had an observation post on duty every evening in an upstairs room of the main building, to report on the movements of this sentry.

From the 14th August, for several days, we were in a very trying position. Daily we had to make up our minds whether we would go out that night and chance the sentry seeing us if he was still on the road, or whether it would be better to wait, hoping the sentry would go into the moat one night before the Germans found out too much.

On the 18th August 1916, at 9.30 p.m., we were about to retire to bed from our customary evening exercise when a message came down from our observation post to say the sentry was in the moat. There was no fuss or commotion of any description. Every one knew where every one else could be found. The exact order in the tunnel had been arranged, and long before 10 p.m. nineteen officers were underneath Campbell's building. There was little to be done here beyond collecting rucksacks, which we had to push along the tunnel in front of us.

In the ordinary course of events we would not be missed till the 9 o'clock roll-call the following morning. As the wind was freshening there was every hope of the sentry remaining in the moat all night, but this of course we had to chance. All prisoners had to remain in their rooms after 10 p.m., which effectively stopped any further information reaching us from the upstairs-room of the main building.

As I lay in the tunnel somewhere in the middle of the party, first I thought Campbell was never going to get through, then some one moving and hitting a side made me think for a moment it was a shot and that the Germans were waiting for us, and that they must have killed Campbell. I suppose it was about 12 midnight before he actually got through.

It was 1 a.m. when I reached the mouth, and the blaze of light from the camp arc lamps was somewhat dazzling at first. It was a great relief to see there was no sentry on the road. There was a heavy drizzle at the time, and as everybody had rolled from the mouth towards the river the pressed-down wet grass already looked like a permanent track.

Originally we had intended to cover our tracks here with pepper, so that when we were missed at the morning roll-call even the camp dogs would not be able to find the mouth of the tunnel.

As there were still several more to roll over the same bit of ground after me, I was quite satisfied that our tracks would be noticed at daybreak at latest.

When Lesaffres joined me at the edge of the river we moved off as fast as we could in a northerly direction. We had only about four more hours of darkness and decided that we must put as much country as we could between us and the camp in that time. My maps showed a large wood about ten miles north of the fortress. This was an obvious objective, for, once reached, cover was assured for the first day.

Soon after reaching the wood we halted for a few minutes. As we lay just off one of the tracks we heard people walking behind us from the direction of the camp. As they passed I recognised Campbell and two Russians, and one of the latter was very startled when I first spoke to them. Lesaffres and myself must have come very fast to catch them up, as they were the first three out. The five of us had some light refreshments together, wished each other the best of luck and then continued in our respective parties.

By daylight Lesaffres and myself had nearly reached the northern extremity of the wood, where we concealed ourselves in obviously excellent cover. It was very damp and soon we were tormented by mosquitoes of the most virulent type.

By midday the wood was full of Germans, some on bikes, some on horses, all tearing up and down the rides, whistling and shouting. They were very active throughout the day, and that they were still present after dark was obvious from the noise they continued to make.

That night we realised the great mistake we had made in going anywhere near that wood. From the camp it had seemed an obvious place to make for. I now realised it was an equally obvious place for the Germans in which to search for some of their nineteen escaped prisoners. I felt we were quite safe in our hiding-place, but I could not see how we were going to get out of it. If we moved along a ride we were certain to walk into a patrol, and the undergrowth in the forest was so thick as to render other movement impossible without making a noise.

Our only chance of remaining at large seemed to be to wait where we were till they had given up the hunt. We were quite prepared to stay there another day, but by 3 a.m. all military activity in the forest appeared to have ceased, and it was with great relief that we managed to get away from the mosquitoes.

It was only possible to make a short march that night and take the best cover available in a small wood a few miles farther north near Ruhlsdorf. It was really bad cover, and this seriously affected our day's rest. The next day, although in rather better cover, we were disturbed by a small boy at 8 a.m., but before he could get assistance we moved about three kilometres farther north in the same wood, covering our tracks with pepper. The next night, our fourth, we came in for a real bad thunderstorm which lasted well into the following day, when we once more found ourselves in an unsatisfactory hiding-place near Lobbese.

We now came to the conclusion that we must pay more attention to seeking good cover, even if it meant shortening our marches considerably.

When walking through the country with Cartwright the previous November the nights were long and there had been ample time in which to conceal ourselves without interfering with the length of the march. Now we could not start walking till after 10 p.m., and we found it advisable to make it a rule to take the first good cover we passed after 3 a.m. It was a little hard to stop at this hour with two hours' more darkness, but during those first few nights we found that good hiding-places were few and far between. If a suitable halting-place had not been reached by 4 a.m. we would then go out of our way to look for one, even, if it meant retracing our steps. This shortened our marches, but we had no further narrow shaves, and were able to enjoy our day's rest all the more. For food we relied mainly on concentrated meat, tinned tunny-fish, biscuits and chocolate, with occasional hot drinks, heated by means of a 'Tommy's cooker.' Sometimes we cooked potatoes, but this we could only do very sparingly, as we had to ration our solid methylated spirits.

One of the reasons for choosing the Baltic in preference to the Dutch frontier was that I did not fancy the idea of crossing the Elbe in summer, as this would necessitate walking over a bridge in broad daylight or waiting till after 10 p.m., when any guard would be certain to ask questions. I did not fancy the idea of swimming so large a river at the commencement of a three hundred mile walk when we were carrying all our provisions. Going north the only river of note to cross was the Havel at Havelberg. The bridge there had not been guarded in November, but even if it were guarded now the river would be easier to swim than the Elbe.

A reconnaisance revealed the fact that the bridge at Havelberg was again unguarded, so Lesaffres disguised himself as a woman and we walked through the town about 11 p.m. one night. We deemed this disguise advisable as Havelberg was the key to the north, and nineteen prisoners escaping from Torgau might easily have caused special precautions to be taken.

During the first eleven days we hid in woods, choosing low pine-trees when available. These afforded excellent cover and were generally in dry soil.

The twelfth day we spent in a barn, which not only gave us excellent cover but also seemed to improve our condition, and for this reason we spent two more days in barns as we neared the end of our journey. On the fifteeneth day we used the barn which I had occupied with Cartwright on the last day of my previous escape.

On the sixteenth day we found excellent cover in a small wood near Bentwick.

On the seventeenth night we followed the road via Rovershagen to Graal, and then went along the coast to Muritz. Between these two places there were about fifteen bathing-places projecting at intervals of a few hundred yards into the sea and surrounded by low concrete walls. We searched each of these hoping to find a small boat such as is frequently used for bathing purposes. We could plainly see the Gjedsor lighthouse in Denmark and a Danish lightship rather more than half-way across the Baltic. We wanted to locate our craft that night and then lie up for the day farther inland and start our sea journey soon after dark the next evening, so as to have the maximum amount of darkness in which to get across.

We could also see the German fishing fleet out about ten miles to our north-east, so if we failed to find a suitable boat where we were we intended to try farther east the following night.

In addition to these bathing-places there were some boat-houses farther inland, but there was no craft of a suitable size in any of them. They were all too big for the two of us to manage or even get to the water's edge.

We were desperately keen to get across the next night. I suppose it was the sight of Denmark added to our great hunger that spurred us on to make the most exhaustive search imaginable. In addition to examining every boat-house, we went into all the fifteen bathing-places, and it was at the very last one of these, outside Muritz, that I walked straight into a sentry. Expecting danger my left hand contained money and my right was full of pepper, the idea being to offer a bribe and if that was not accepted to hurl a handful of pepper in the sentry's face and run for liberty. The sentry would be almost certain to take the money and let us go, but if not, after he had received a handful of pepper in his face he most certainly would not see to shoot us as we ran away. It was with such confidence that we approached all these bathing-places. Just as I was starting to negotiate with the sentry his relief was marched up by an under-officer. There were now three of them, so there was nothing we could do but allow ourselves to be marched to their guard-room.

It is easy to say now that, after seeing the coast, we should have gone inland and later visited one or two other portions of the coast before taking the risks we took that night. Undoubtedly we should, but it was my belief at the time that every day we spent in the country was an additional risk which was greater than the risk we took that night. It was possibly arriving there in a tired, hungry and perhaps excited condition that made me look on it in that light at the time. With the rations we still had we could have kept ourselves alive for another week, and I am sure on this occasion we made the same mistake as many other escaping prisoners had done by rushing things too much when nearing our goal.

It was bad luck meeting a sentry the moment when he was being relieved, but it is always bad luck which causes the prisoner to be recaptured. The escaping prisoner does not want luck to assist him—he just hopes to avoid having bad luck. There are so many different things that might go wrong and lead to his recapture, and the odds are that something unexpected will occur sooner or later.

We were recaptured about 3.30 a.m. on the 4th September 1916 and, after being roughly handled in the guard-room at Muritz, were made to walk to Warnemunde, where we were kept under special guard in an hotel for thirty-six hours. Escape would have been difficult as we were in a room on the top story of the building and were made to leave the door open, the sentry stopping in the doorway day and night.

We were both so bitterly disappointed with the result of our search on the coast that we really had not the inclination to try a further escape up there and decided to wait till we were taken back to Torgau and then try to get to Holland or Switzerland.

On 7th September we were brought back to Torgau via Berlin, where we had to change stations. As we refused to pay for a cab this necessitated a walk through the town past the Hindenburg monument. It was rather amusing to see all the motor-cars in the streets with spring rims instead of rubber tyres, and those in showrooms with wooden tyres painted to look like rubber. Confectioners' shop windows were full of large chocolate boxes containing nothing. All this was part of a specially organised scheme to try and prevent the German public from realising the serious shortage the war was causing.

On arrival at Torgau we were brought to a civil prison, not to the military one where I had been before. Here we found all the rest of the tunnellers except one French officer who was walking to Holland by himself. This officer had heard of the tunnel at the last moment and begged to be allowed to go. I gave him all my maps to Holland, including the one with the position of the two sentries, and I heard afterwards that he succeeded after thirty-five days and was subsequently killed at Salonika. The superstitious ones amongst us put our misfortunes down to having started on a Friday.

Although eighteen of us had been recaptured, it is interesting to note that no one was caught within fifty miles of Torgau.

The civil prison here was already fairly full with German civilian criminals, and it was only possible to allot us accommodation in the top flat, where we were kept two in a cell, with the exception of a large one at the end of the passage which held four. At first I shared a small cell with a Russian, but later I was moved to the larger one, which I shared with Campbell, Graham-Toler and a Russian. All the cells looked on to a small exercising yard twenty-five yards by ten yards. There was no feasible exit from here and at night a dog was left in it.

Our jailer did his best to make our stay as comfortable as possible; in the evenings he used to let us visit other cells to play cards or talk, but he would not accept any bribes, so we had to think of other means of escaping. A long term of imprisonment seemed inevitable, so using my invisible ink, I at once wrote home for metal saws, acid and files, sending new instructions as to how they were to be sent. I also studied the art of picking locks, practising first with small ones on boxes and on padlocks, which I soon discovered were very much more difficult than the larger ones on doors.

In due course my tools arrived and were a very fine set. The saw was of such dimensions that I imagined it would be possible to cut a hole in the ceiling one night and thus escape through the roof and down the farther side of the prison into a small yard separated from the main street by a large double door, not a formidable obstacle to tackle from the inside. Campbell and Graham-Toler agreed to come with me, and we started collecting kit. We decided to go to Switzerland, and, owing to the distance, clothes fit to be seen in walking through towns were essential. Anyhow, we had to be sufficiently well dressed to be able to walk out of the town of Torgau. Collecting these clothes gave us great difficulty.

Meanwhile the camp authorities were very active in their attempts to get what information they could out of us in connection with the tunnel. They failed to get an admission of responsibility from anyone, even Campbell. The usual charge against prisoners, who were caught tunnelling, was 'damage to Government property,' but in this case there was no evidence as to who was responsible for the damage. Interviews, both in the prison and in the camp Commandant's office, seemed to increase as time went on. I suppose work there had just about reached its maximum towards the end of November when we were warned that we were to be tried on a charge of 'mutiny' on the 8th December. The news was broken to us with much ceremony by the Commandant himself, who came down in person to see what effect it would have on us. At the end of the address, when he asked if we had anything to say, Campbell asked if he could be given permission to buy champagne in order to celebrate St. Andrew's Day in our cell. During the next five minutes I quite expected to see the Commandant explode. It was difficult not to laugh whenever we saw this official, for we learnt in prison that he had been awarded an Iron Cross two days before we escaped for keeping his camp intact for so long; and that the announcement had appeared in the papers for the first time the day after our departure, when it was inserted immediately following a full account of the escape.

At the court martial the prosecution opened by reading out from a dictionary the definition of the word 'mutiny,' i.e. 'When two or more people unite and use force to overthrow authority.' It was then claimed that we must have used force to propel ourselves along the tunnel. Witnesses of all nationalities were produced, and as each gave evidence in his own language it was interpreted into three others before he was cross-examined by the nineteen prisoners in turn. The interpreters got so confused that it really didn't matter very much what the prisoners said, and some, no doubt, were guilty of contempt of court. Frequently, after a harmless remark by a prisoner, the interpreter would make a muddle of things, with the result that the members of the court would all suddenly flare up and adjourn to decide whether the statement was to be treated as contempt of court. After an interval sufficiently long for the consumption of light refreshments (by the Court), the Court would reappear, announce that they considered it was contempt of court, and would then continue. The prisoners were kept in court the whole day without food.

After a verdict of guilty, Campbell was awarded seven months, and the remainder six months in prison—to start from the date of trial. The imprisonment we had already done was not to count. We all claimed the right to appeal, remembering that Templer, who had not done so after his trial at Burg, had had his sentence of six months increased to one year by the army commander.

On the 13th December 1916 we were told that we were to be moved the following day. Campbell and Graham-Toler had not got sufficient clothes for an escape, but I decided to try and cut my way through the ceiling that night.

No matter what our necessities we were not allowed out of our cells between 9 p.m. and 8 a.m., so provided no undue noise was made, there was little chance of interruption between those hours. After removing the plaster I sawed away at the beams all night, but until I had started I had no idea of the magnitude of the work I had undertaken, and I failed to complete the job before daylight.

The jailer found us all apparently asleep at 8 a.m., and as he continued to examine the damage in silence we suddenly all burst out laughing, and he himself quite saw the humour of the situation. The camp authorities did little on arrival, as they were really so relieved at the thought of getting rid of us that day.

Lesaffres and four Russians were sent to the civil prison at Burg, while the four English and eight Russian officers were ordered to Magdeburg.

I was frequently on the look-out for an opportunity to jump off the train, but my fatigue and the careful supervision of the guard caused the journey to be uneventful.

IV

HALLE AND MAGDEBURG

By H. A. CARTWRIGHT

Camp at Halle—Removal to Fürstenberg—Back to Burg—Hiding-places for contraband—Removal to Magdeburg—Sawing bars and forging passes—Walking out of camp with Marshall—Doing the sights of Berlin—By train across Germany—Crossing the Emms—Recapture on the frontier at Neu Süstrum—Return to Magdeburg—How stores were received from home—The parcels room—'Escape' parcels.

IN my account of our walk to Rostock from Burg I told how Harrison and I were deliberately separated after our recapture, and I now have to tell shortly of my movements while the events which he has described in the last chapter were taking place.

I arrived at Halle on the 29th December 1915. Halle was even farther than Burg from the Dutch frontier and not much nearer to Switzerland. The camp was a very strong one, composed of a group of more or less derelict factory buildings surrounding a scrap yard, and was in the middle of the town. It was a large one, and I met there several Frenchmen and one Britisher—Hardy, of the Connaught Rangers, one of the 'maniacs,' who had been sent there for safe custody after breaking out from other camps—and my knowledge of outside conditions was much increased by what they told me.

I began with another British officer to plan a walk to Holland, and we collected a fairly good set of maps and all the other necessary stores, but never hit on anything like a probable way of getting out of the camp. Only one prisoner—the 'maniac'—got out of Halle while I was there. His was a one-man scheme, involving the very quick picking of three or four locks in the German staff quarters and a nerve-racking crawl over several roofs in full view of the guard, but it came off without a hitch. The nature of the escape made it impossible for him to carry an adequate supply of food and clothing, and he was caught a few days later trying to stow away on a goods train, in a more or less starving condition.

I was still looking for a way out when we English were all moved from the camp on the 1st June 1916. The Germans had discovered that the place was an ideal ready-made reprisal camp, so they filled it up with selected Frenchmen on whom they wanted to practice a little *kultur* by way of reply to the reported (no doubt correctly) lack of home comforts in the prisoners' camps in France.

I went with a small party to Fürstenberg, a small health-resort to the north of Berlin, farther than ever from the land frontiers but nearer to the Baltic and not far from the country through which Harrison and I had walked on our way to Rostock. The quarters here were in a real dwelling-house—the only one I lived in during nearly four years in

Germany—quite obviously too good for English pig-dogs, so, on the 4th July we were all turned out to make room for a gang of Poles, Jews, Baltic Germans, Ukrainians and various other brands of disloyal Russians whom the Germans thought they might fatten up and make use of. The camp was an easy one to break out of and I was preparing with a very keen conspirator for another walk to the Baltic when we were moved without notice just before our plans were ready.

I was sent, with about thirty other Englishmen, back to Burg-bei-Magdeburg. The camp authorities received me coldly and I expected to be passed on without delay, especially as many of those who had helped in my last departure from the camp were still there. My baggage contained many carefully concealed maps, compasses, wire-cutters, electric torches, etc., so I unpacked only the necessary pyjamas and tooth-brush and left everything else packed and ready for the expected move. After five days, however, the British officer who acted as interpreter learnt from one of the German interpreters that the Commandant had asked for instructions to send me back to Halle, where the camp had been opened again to all nationalities, but had been told that he must keep me. I therefore unpacked my baggage and opened up the hiding-places of some of my contraband for the purpose of swopping part of it with another prisoner.

I had barely finished when the Germans came in and told me to get ready to move in an hour. I had to bundle everything in as quickly as I could, hoping that, since I had been very carefully searched on arrival only five days before, I might get off unsearched; but this was not to be; I was very thoroughly put through it and lost more of my half-hidden stuff than I had lost in a dozen previous visitations. They got two pairs of wire-cutters, a file, a pair of civilian trousers, a cap, some German money and a copied map on which I had worked for three months at Halle and which showed the whole of the Dutch frontier and every village and track eastwards as far as Hanover. In the Prussian camps the prisoners were given tokens instead of money for use in the canteens, but at Fürstenberg we had used the ordinary paper currency, and I had collected some hundreds of marks for future use. They didn't get it all.

This brings me to the subject of hiding forbidden stores, on which I must say a few words.

It would be impossible to give anything like a complete description of the many and varied devices by which forbidden articles were kept hidden, but I will mention a few which I used myself.

We had to be prepared at all times for the sudden entry into our rooms of searching parties, composed generally of officers and under-officers but often consisting—in the Magdeburg Army Corps Area—of detectives. Whether officers, under-officers, trained customs searchers or detectives, they were generally perfectly harmless.

When moving from one camp to another our baggage and persons were always put through a search—which, in the case of those with a bad record at least, was intended to be very thorough—both on leaving the old camp and on arrival at the new. When I later left Küstrin for Schweidnitz my baggage was, of course, searched—with no result. I was myself stripped naked and searched by two officers while my clothing was gone through by an alleged tailor; nevertheless I retained possession of a small compass which I wanted to keep on me in case I found an opportunity of dropping off the train.

I possessed at different times a small cabin trunk, a packing-case, a thing like a chorus girl's basket, and an assortment of cardboard suit-cases. They were kept always stuffed quite full of clothing, books, letters, cooking, washing and feeding utensils, and all the other assortment of rubbish which prisoners used to accumulate.

The receptacles themselves always had one or more hiding-places which the searchers never even nearly discovered, no matter what their training. The cabin trunk, for instance, had the usual light linen tray. I used to keep maps stitched to the underside of it with an extra layer of linen under them. This would seem fairly easy for the searchers, but I used to help them by packing all the things they had examined into one end of the tray as they handed them back to me; then, when they had finished that layer, I used helpfully to lift out the tray so that they could get on with the stuff underneath without getting mixed.

The packing-case had a large false back. They knew about false bottoms and used knowingly to measure the depth inside and outside. They could see that the sides were solid and the back was partly

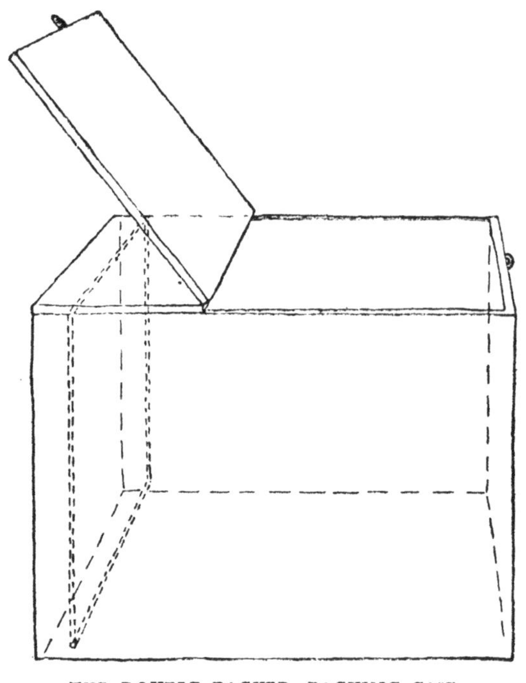

THE DOUBLE-BACKED PACKING-CASE

hidden by the cover. A few sharp nails turned inwards used to discourage them from messing about too much under the cover and they drew blood every time. I used the box for two years with complete success. It often held maps of the whole of Germany, money, compasses, torches, passes, tools and a gent's trilby hat. It was searched dozens of times.

The main ribs of the basket were detachable and hollow and contained quite a large sum in notes. The slats under the bottom held a lot.

I hid money, passes, the smaller sections of maps, compasses, etc., at different times in tins of boot polish, the backs of brushes (prized off, hollowed out and restuck with glue), tooth-paste tubes, shaving-soap (they tumbled to the last two at Magdeburg and ran needles through them but they used sharp needles and failed to notice the bank-notes—I don't know what they expected to feel—and after that we only put in such things as five-pfennig pieces, which they were bound to find ; this made them feel clever and they liked it), safety-razor handles and the padded lining of their cases, spectacle-cases, book-covers, cap-peaks and dozens of other articles of everyday use. They always looked down the backs of books, but never discovered that the cardboard covers could be split, filled with notes or maps and the linen closed up with glue without leaving a mark.

I had also a drawing-board measuring about one foot by eighteen inches. I used to keep half a dozen unfinished sketches of unpleasant-looking—but not libellously so—Germans pinned on it. The searchers used to take all the sketches off and look at both sides of the paper and swear at my style of art, but it never occurred to them that the board itself was worthy of attention. It was made of ply-wood with edges of solid deal, one of which moved in a grove, and it held quite a lot of maps, money, and papers. It was made by a Russian with only a pocket-knife and some sand-paper.

At Küstrin the rooms occupied by the British were all provided with receptacles in which supplies could be kept after being unpacked while their more permanent hiding-places were being got ready and into which anything unhidden could be hastily thrown on the (always obvious) approach of a searching party. In one room the lining of a doorway was made to hinge back to give access to a large hole, as big as a small wardrobe, hollowed out of the thickness of the wall. In another the window frame hid a similar receptacle, and in all there were moving bits of skirting-board, etc., with useful holes behind them. The Germans used to search the furniture and lift loose floor-boards (a few of which were always provided to keep them occupied) but they never thought of looking higher up.

By far the safest hiding-place was the parcels room—where the Germans kept all food-tins until such time as we wanted them, when they would decant them and rake through the contents—and we always kept most of our surplus stores there—in sealed tins. There were plenty of experts who could resolder a carefully opened tin, and replace the labels without leaving a mark. This was particularly useful before a move, since the tins were simply transferred from custody in one camp into custody in the other without any examination. How we removed the tins, uncensored, from the parcels room, and placed there the tins in which we had hidden our stores, will appear later; but for the moment I must get on with the story.

My destination this time was Magdeburg, where I arrived the same afternoon, 10th July 1916, and it was there that I discovered for the first time with what horror an 'escape maniac' could be looked on by a certain small group of prisoners. One of the 'maniacs' had actually escaped a few days before, and there had been some risk of an officer suspected (most unjustly) of helping him being sent to prison for three days—where he would have been, almost certainly, deprived of his fret-working outfit. This state of affairs made things a little difficult, and it was not until October that I began seriously to make plans again on the arrival of a French officer who wanted to make an attempt. This officer, Lieutenant Marshall, was a flying officer of some distinction who had been captured by the Austrians and, for some reason of high policy which he never fathomed, handed over by them to the Germans. He was an Alsatian, and, having lived in Berlin for some eight years up to the outbreak of war, spoke German perfectly and was confident of being able to pass as a native.

The camp was well wired and heavily guarded. It consisted of two parts, one a range of gun-sheds and mobilisation stores known as the Wagenhaus, the other an old fort dating from Napoleonic days. Each was in its own barbed wire enclosure, connected one with the other by a wired gangway. The prisoners were all shut into the buildings after dark. Marshall lived in the Scharnhorst—the old fort—and I lived in one of the store-rooms, so that we could not communicate after dark. Secrecy was more than ever essential.

Bath-rooms in German camps were generally cellars with a number of squirts in the ceiling. The prisoners stood in dense crowds under the squirts and practised communal washing. Sometimes there was a tin bath in an adjoining cellar, for which the competition was very hot. The first plan we hit on was to cut a bar of the window of the Scharnhorst bathroom. We would then hide under the coal in the stoke-hole, get locked in and after dark climb out of the window which opened on the moat. It would then be possible to crawl along the moat and get on to a line of railway, and so away from the camp without passing too close to any of the known sentries. The possibility of unknown sentries being posted after dark had to be chanced. We should have to pass one post at close quarters, but sooner or later its sentry was sure to stroll over to the next post, and we hoped to have the whole night from which to choose the right moment. I had two compasses, a very fine set of motor maps, newly acquired from home, and plenty of German money. Marshall's knowledge of Germany and of the language made him thoroughly confident of being able to get us both safely through a railway journey—given ordinary luck.

We acquired two metal saws and began to work on the window bar. I could not risk being found in the bathroom, having no right to be in that part of the Scharnhorst, so had to leave all the work to Marshall. By the time he was half through the bar both saws were out of action and we had to hunt for more. We made quite good ones from gramophone springs and got on slowly with the work. At the same time we were trying to make false keys for the bathroom door; these, by allowing Marshall to work when the bathroom was officially closed, would have saved a great deal of time. As things were he could only work very short shifts, since, when it was open, there was almost always some one in the room, and he had to be content with a few strokes of the saw whenever he was alone. When not at work he filled the cut in the bar with plasticine.

By the middle of December we were nearly ready when the Elbe suddenly came down in flood and put five or six feet of water into the moat through which we proposed to crawl. At the same time the Germans somehow stumbled—led to it, we believed, by a certain Russian—on the sawn bar, repaired it, and put a soldier permanently on duty in the bathroom.

We had intended to depart on Christmas Day, counting on many of the guard being drunk or at least torpid. If we were delayed, New Year's Day would do nearly as well for the same reason.

We now decided that the only thing to be done was for Marshall to dress as a German officer and march me out of the camp in my own uniform, as if he were taking me to prison or to another camp.

The beauty of this scheme was its novelty. We knew it had never been tried, therefore there could be no orders on the subject, and without orders the German is paralysed. If a sentry saw a German officer marching a prisoner out of the camp there was no reason why he should be very much astonished, and he would be most unlikely to dare to object.

With the practice I had had at Burg I rather fancied myself as a tailor, and the uniform for Marshall presented no difficulty. I made the great-coat from a Russian one which happened to be of almost exactly the right shade. We added a rich-looking fur collar made from the lining of Marshall's flying coat. His cap was a real German one, given, minus badges, to a British officer who had lost his own in some hospital near the front. It was very dirty, but I took it to the bath with me every week.

We should have to pass two sentries whose duty it was to examine the papers of all coming in or going out of the camp. Officers of the camp staff carried yellow passes with their photographs on them. It was impossible to obtain one of these for copying purposes, so I had to make something that would be even more impressive. I made it foolscap size and covered it with large printed headings, in Gothic type, such as 'War Ministry,' 'Date,' 'Department,' 'Number,' etc., and dotted it all over with rubber stamp impressions (which are very easily forged) such as delight the heart of the German in authority and fill the private soldier with awe. Marshall filled it in in German script and we stuck on it a photograph of a German in a uniform very like his. I found the photograph on the piano in a dentist's waiting-room. The finished article was something like the one illustrated, and was finished off with passable forgeries of the signatures of all the local Jacks-in-office. The printing on the original, being done when I was a prisoner and had unlimited time at my disposal, was much better than on the specimen opposite, which was made roughly from memory after I came home. The photograph on the original was not quite so idealised as the one illustrated.

Germans, whether officers or not, who took prisoners out of the camp carried also a gelatine-printed document, on which was entered the number and description of the prisoners passed out on it. The gate sentries were supposed to read this and check the prisoners, to see if they tallied with the number entered on it.

To get a copy of this document I had to make a number of malingering visits to dentists, oculists, ear specialists, etc., each time getting a look at the paper, but never until the last time being able actually to get hold of one. On that occasion my escort tore up and threw away the pass as soon as we were inside the camp, but it was after dark, so I was taken straight to my building and locked up without having a chance of collecting the bits.

Next morning I was out very early, although there were several inches of snow on the ground, for a run round the yard in pyjamas, when I was suddenly seized with an irresistible desire to make a snowball. Much to the amusement of the gate sentry I did so, and collected every scrap of paper in the ball. I carried it past the guard, who roared with laughter at the mad pig-dog, and up to my room, where I melted the snow and found that I had got the whole pass without missing a scrap. I pieced the bits together and, with the aid of a gelatine outfit which was used by a Belgian musician for printing concert programmes, made an exact copy of the original. I filled it in with Marshall's name in the space for the escorting German and gave him the rank of *Leutnant der Reserve.* In the space for prisoners I put my own name and rank.

Provided with these two papers it was unlikely that any sentry would put up a serious resistance to our exit; if he were to be officious, Marshall could curse him and shout him down just as well as any German.

I ought here to mention that in Germany during the war every man, woman and child carried some kind of pass or identity paper, and later on we found it possible to produce forgeries of these which were quite capable of passing—in a crowd—the cursory examination of a policeman or gendarme at a railway station or street barrier. The genuine articles were local productions, issued by the police or military authorities, so that there was no standard pattern and almost any design would be accepted provided it was not shown in the district in which it was supposed to have been issued.

Generally the pass consisted of a card or slip of paper with a heading of some sort at the top and sub-headings against which were filled in the name, trade, age, sex, personal description, etc., of the bearer—in fact, they gave most of the information usually given in a passport, and a few words were generally written across the document to authorise any journey outside the bearer's own district. They were stamped and counterstamped all over with impressions of the rubber seals so dear to the official German and signed with a mass of elaborate flourishes. To forge printed Latin characters with a pen and ink would be nearly impossible, but it was comparatively easy to copy the German Gothic type with a mapping pen and Indian ink and unlimited time—the one commodity always at the prisoner's disposal.

There were experts who cut very passable rubber stamps on any bits of india-rubber which came handy, their tools being splinters of safety-razor blades, but I preferred to paint the forgeries directly on to the paper with a brush. Wet blotting-paper well rubbed with indelible pencil or soaked in red ink made a perfectly good pad.

Another method was to draw the stamp reversed in indelible pencil, wet it and transfer it to the forged document. There were always men who could fill in the manuscript part in good German script.

The documents which Marshall carried when he marched me out of the Magdeburg camp were much more elaborate than those described above, and I have no doubt that they would have failed to arouse suspicion had we bumped into a sentry who was officious enough to read them through. The big document was an original composition, but the smaller one was in everyday use and was quite enough by itself; he only carried the larger one because it was safer to show something imposing, if unusual, than to invent an officers' identity card when there might be, for all we knew, a stereotyped pattern for the whole army. The civilians' cards which we made later were unknown to us at that time, otherwise we should have used them instead of dodging the 'Kontrols' at Bremen and Oldenburg.[1]

The paper which I showed at Neu Bruchausen [2] undoubtedly satisfied the imbeciles who examined it, and I believe they would have let us go if Harrison could have produced his, though they were a bit astonished at finding Belgians wandering loose about the country. Forged identity papers were used by several others with complete success, although put to much more severe tests than any which I manufactured.

[1] See p. 137. [2] See Chapter V.

By the time Marshall and I were ready a frost had set in, which proved the most severe, and one of the longest, recorded in Germany for over thirty years. This suited us well, since we intended to try to cross the Dutch frontier between Meppen and Pappenburg, and the chief obstacle in that sector is the river Emms. We knew that all ferries and bridges were guarded, but we could now count on the river being frozen and could cross it wherever we liked. We reckoned on lying up for two days only, so could take plenty of food and warm clothing.

We planned to go by train to some point sixty or seventy kilometres (about forty miles) from the frontier and walk the rest of the way.

On 26th January 1917, at about 4.40 p.m., Marshall and I met in one of the ground-floor rooms of the Scharnhorst. We were dressed in civilian jackets and trousers of sorts and wore celluloid collars. The civilian clothing was not difficult to collect since many of the Belgian officers had nothing else; it had been dotted over with buttons, patches, stripes, etc., by the Germans, but these were easily removed or concealed. Marshall had on a civilian overcoat and over that his German military great-coat, the whole outfit being covered again (fortunately he was a very small man) by an English Burberry. His trousers were tucked into yellow leggings and he wore a wooden sword. I wore a civilian overcoat, made from an English soldier's great-coat of the obsolete dark grey pattern, my service dress cap, puttees and a khaki

Burberry over the lot; to all appearances I was in English uniform.

We walked out of the Scharnhorst and joined a small group of officers who were lounging outside a hut, used by a messing committee of Germans and Belgians, about fifty yards from the gate. There we had to wait a few minutes until certain

'ALL CORRECT'

sentries, who overlooked the spot, were reported to be walking their beats with their backs towards us.

One after the other the English officers who were watching them gave the word 'Right!' and on the instant Marshall's outer covering of Burberry was ripped off him, his German cap was put on his head and a small portmanteau was pushed into my hand. The moment the change was effected we walked off towards the main gate. Just as we reached it an Englishman, an old friend of mine, ran after us, shook my hand and begged me to write soon and often, at which Marshall turned round and screamed curses at me in the true Prussian manner. The first sentry only glanced at the papers, which Marshall held out under his face, and passed us out. Fifty yards farther on a second sentry also passed us out with no more than a casual glance at the papers. Provided we met no one belonging to the camp itself we were safe for the moment, and we walked as quickly as we dared towards a public park which lies just outside the city wall.

In the first quiet street I bent to do up a boot-lace and when I straightened up I was wearing a brown felt hat instead of my uniform cap. In the dusk my Burberry was much like any other raincoat and my puttees were unnoticeable. With no English pig-dog to draw attention to him Marshall fitted perfectly into the picture as an inconspicuous German officer. Once in the park, which was almost deserted, we began as we walked to strip Marshall of his glory. He broke and threw away the sword and cap and folded the great-coat over his arm. We walked on throwing a bit here and there whenever we found ourselves alone, and in this way got rid of the fur collar, shoulder-straps, leggings, buttons, etc., and my puttees and tore up and scattered the papers. Outside the town, when it was quite dark, we went into some allotments and tore up and threw away the remains of the great-coat.

We opened the portmanteau and took out two rucksacks (every man, woman and child in Germany carries a rucksack) and put my Burberry into the former. Two soldiers who suddenly appeared, approaching quite silently over the snow, gave us the shock of our lives, but they fled the moment they saw us, evidently even more frightened than we were. They were probably potato thieves out to burgle some of the huts which were scattered over the allotments. Potatoes at that time (January 1917) were already the staple diet of the poorer classes.

The transformation complete, we started for the station—two poor but honest Huns of the working class. We stopped once more in the park while Marshall bound a bandage all over my ears and mouth, leaving only a small hole for food to be pushed through. It was obvious to anyone then that I could not speak, and must be more or less deaf.

The times and destinations of all trains are as clearly indicated at big German stations as they are in a London tube, and the traveller need never buy a time-table or ask a question. As soon as we entered the station we saw that a fast train was leaving for Berlin in a few minutes. We had decided to take the first train in any direction so as to get as far as possible from Magdeburg before we were missed. Berlin was an excellent jumping-off place and an easy one to hide in, so Marshall booked us, third class, for that city, and we went on to the platform.

The train was very full and we had to stand in the corridor with a crowd of soldiers and women. I looked as sick as I could and shook my head and pointed to Marshall whenever anyone spoke to me. He chatted to every one near him, and, when anyone asked him what was the matter with me, hinted darkly at a terrible explosion in a munition factory, about which it was *streng verboten* to speak. The women jabbered continually of food and how to swindle the food-controllers and make strawberry jam out of turnips, the soldiers of the horrors of the war in France and of ingenious frauds by means of which it was said to be possible to get sent to one of the other fronts. They were immensely tickled by a notice which was posted all over the corridor and compartments and which read—'*Vorsicht bei Sprechen. Spionengefahr!*' ('Careful what you say. Spy danger!')

We were due in Berlin at 9 p.m., but the train was snowed up for a couple of hours and did not reach the Potsdamer station until 11 p.m.

Oldenburg—via Bremen—was to be our first point, so we walked over to the Lehrter station to see when we could get a train, and found that the first for Bremen left at 4.15 a.m. We did not care to hang about the station for four or five hours, not knowing if the hunt was up (we might have been missed at the 10 p.m. inspection, at which the prisoners were counted like roosting chickens), so we decided to walk about the streets all night. Marshall knew every inch of Berlin.

WE MUST HAVE LOOKED MORE CONVINCING GERMANS THAN THIS, BUT THIS IS WHAT WE FELT LIKE!

We hid our packs under some rhododendrons in a public garden and walked about in the most crowded streets. Marshall showing me all the sights of the city. We visited the Reichstag, several imperial palaces, all the theatres and the wooden

Hindenburg, for which last Marshall insisted on showing his contempt as only a good Frenchman would. I had the greatest difficulty in keeping him on the move in Friedrichstrasse and Unter den Linden, where every other building seemed to hold memories of pre-war gallantries. He was furious at the amount of light displayed all over the town as compared with the darkened streets of Paris, the more so because he had been captured on a flight during which he had dropped leaflets over Berlin to demonstrate that the French, if they were not such little gentlemen, could bomb the city just as easily as the Germans could bomb Paris.

It was too cold to sit or stand about, and we were very tired by the time we got back to the Lehrter Bahnhof. Our carriage was crowded all the way, and the train stopped at every station between Berlin and Bremen, but we got into no difficulty and managed to sleep a good deal. It was the Kaiser's birthday, flags were hung out everywhere, and every one in the train was wondering what he, the Kaiser, would have to eat.

In order to avoid the station barriers at Bremen, where there might have been a 'Kontrol' (inspection of identity papers by police or gendarmes), we left the train at a small suburban station and went on into the town by tram. We walked a little and then took a cab and drove about for an hour, getting a meal from my portmanteau, which we had not dared to open in the train because the food in it was packed in English tins and boxes.

We left Bremen at about 5 p.m. by another stopping train and arrived at Oldenburg at about 7.30.

We had thought of leaving the railway altogether here, but a 'Kontrol' was in full blast at the barriers, so we decided to go on to Cloppenburg, a small town about sixty kilometres from the Emms and seventy from the frontier, a train being due out in a few minutes. Paying the excess fare on the train presented no difficulties to Marshall.

Between Oldenburg and Cloppenburg my ignorance of the language nearly got us into difficulties. There were few travellers and we had the carriage to ourselves, when, just as Marshall had gone to the lavatory compartment, we stopped at a small station. There was some shouting and a female conductor or guard threw open the door of our carriage, bellowed something at me and passed on. I took no notice, but presently she came back with a man and in no uncertain tone they called me unkind things and ordered me to get out. Fortunately Marshall returned in the nick of time and took charge of the situation. The lady had told me, at her first call, that the coach was on fire, so perhaps their irritation at my calmness was not unnatural. An axle had heated and set fire to the floor-boards. The coach was uncoupled and shunted and we continued the journey in another empty compartment.

At about 9.30 p.m. we got out at a small village just short of Cloppenburg. We went into a wood close to the station, took our compasses from the dubbin tins in which they had been hidden and the maps from the false bottom of a cigar-box, repacked our rucksacks and abandoned the portmanteau. Marshall had poured the dubbin hot on to his compass and this had caused the card to curl up and made it quite useless—an accident which let us down badly later on.

We tried to skirt Cloppenburg, but the going, in deep snow, was too bad, and we had to go through the town and strike out on the main road to the west. It was a good road but the surface was in bad condition having been first cut up by sleighs and then frozen hard. We covered about thirty kilometres before dawn, when we turned into a plantation of small pines to lie up for the day. We spread pine branches on the snow, laid my Burberry on them, put on extra shirts, two or three cardigans, and several pairs of socks, lay down as close together as possible and from sheer weariness got about an hour's sleep. The day's lie-up was not comfortable, but, thanks to the hard frost, we kept perfectly dry ; we should have been much worse off had the temperature been rather higher and the snow under us moist. The moisture from our feet formed a thin layer of ice over our socks—of course we took off our boots—and this seemed to have the effect of keeping our feet almost warm

After the first hour we made no attempt to sleep but spent the day brewing oxo and cocoa and eating, almost continuously.

We moved on at about 5 p.m., skirting all the villages we came to before midnight. Very few people were about. The going became worse. When we were getting near the Emms we left the road and tried to follow a light railway, but this got us rather into difficulties, since we could not find the road again when we wanted to. At dawn we could find only the thinnest of cover, but the bad going had nearly finished us, so we had to lie down and chance it. We slept for about an hour and woke up to find good cover—another plantation of young pines—quite close by, so we moved into it and spent another day exactly like the last.

We broke cover at about 6 p.m. and made across country, by compass, for cross-roads about three kilometres from the river, which were to be our starting-point. We found the cross-roads at 8 p.m. and at the same time a very bright moon appeared from behind a cloud-bank and lit up the snow-covered country very much too brightly for our liking. We decided not to attempt to cross the river while the moon was up, and spent the next four and a half hours walking up and down the road, disappearing discreetly into cover when anyone approached—which happened only twice. There was a biting east wind, and—although we wore every scrap of extra clothing which we had brought for the lie-up—it was too cold to sit down for more than a couple of minutes at a time, and my moustache was a solid mass of ice. We knew that we should have very little to fear from frontier sentries on such a night, but we had plenty of time for the short distance to the frontier, and we made up our minds to neglect no precaution.

At about 1 a.m. the moon set and we began cautiously to approach the Emms. We had to cross a road and a railway and then a narrow belt of forest, from the far side of which we expected to see the river. Going through the wood so close to the frontier was rather a jumpy business, and we could not help expecting a sentry to bark at us from behind every tree, although we knew perfectly well that if we came on one he would have his back to the wind and all his wife's woollen garments swathed round his ears and we should see him long before he heard us. From the far side of the wood we found, instead of the river, what appeared to be a field of ice, partly cleared of snow by the wind, stretching as far as we could see. We started to cross this, going due west by compass. Sometimes we walked on solid ice, many inches thick; at other times we found ourselves on cat-ice, where the water had fallen away after forming only a thin layer of ice, and here each step made a report like a gun as we crashed through on to the grass or a second or third layer of ice below. Sometimes the surface was good and level; at other times, owing to the water having gone from under a thick layer, it was bent into long slopes, unnoticeable in the dark, until one suddenly found oneself slipping backwards. But where there was a slope there were generally cracks, and we could get along by working round the edges of these. When we were crashing through the cat-ice we expected every minute to attract a patrol, but although, as we found out next morning, the country was thick with soldiers—of a sort—we neither saw nor heard any sign of them.

Half a dozen times we thought we had crossed the river. After what seemed to be about a mile of ice we were held up by a deep drain running north and south with several layers of cat-ice over it, but nothing which would bear our weight. We had to follow it for a mile or more, southwards, at right angles to our proper direction, before we found a way across. Shortly after this we really crossed the Emms; it was quite unmistakable, being a mass of jammed ice-blocks quite unlike the smooth surface of the flooded marshes.

A hundred yards from the river I suddenly went through the ice. I had fallen into another deep drain exactly like the one which had given us so much trouble on the other side of the river except that this one was hidden by snow. The level of the water had been continually falling all through the frost so that there were six or eight layers of thin ice, and, finally, water. I was in water up to my middle and could get no support anywhere, since wherever I put my hands they fell on thin ice which broke away immediately. I was so numbed after a few minutes that I could do little to help myself. Marshall had stopped when he heard the crash, and called out to know what had happened. I told him not to come near me but to get a rail or something and fish me out. He misunderstood me, came too close and crashed down on top of me. He fell, however, partly on the bank with only his feet in the water and managed to get a grip of some willow branches with his left hand. He stood about five feet three inches, but was as strong as an ox. He got hold of my coat and, pulling himself up by the willow branches, dragged me up the bank. I was none the worse for the bathe but much colder than I ever want to be again. We had made a terrific din but had not apparently succeeded in waking any of the sentries.

We found a way across the drain and started off again due west by the compass, which I had held in my hand all the time.

We crossed about another mile of ice and then had what seemed to be open fields and rough moorlands before us. The east wind was still blowing strongly, with a little snow in it, and once more we felt confident that there was small chance of any sentry being in the open if he could find any sort of cover. It was altogether an ideal night for crossing the frontier. The next day we saw a sentry brought in who had died at his post in the night, frozen stiff. In spite of official jeering at the blockade, the German home-service soldier's ration did not provide much of a cold-resisting diet.

We went at a slow trot—a very slow one, since we were travelling over rough grass with a foot of snow on it—most of the way, keeping always to the open and avoiding all buildings, trees, bushes or anything which might conceivably cover a German, and only stopping to look at the compass, which had a luminous dial. I carried the compass and Marshall kept about fifty yards away from me so that, if one of us blundered into a sentry or patrol the other would have a good chance of getting away. We had to cross a few wire fences, one or two frozen canals or big drains and some deep and narrow dry ditches.

My trousers and the skirts of my overcoat and Burberry had frozen stiff after my wetting, and the swishing and rattling of the latter seemed to us loud enough to wake the dead.

We had no means of knowing exactly when we were at the frontier, but we knew it to be seven kilometres west of the Emms at the point where we thought we had crossed it. When it began to get light, at 7.30 a.m., we calculated that we could not have travelled much less than five kilometres an hour and must be about twelve kilometres on the right side of the frontier.

We rejoiced accordingly—Marshall was Frenchman enough to embrace me—and finished our food.

During this last night Marshall had prevailed on me to swallow some kind of drug, which he had in tablet form. I forget what he called it, but I know that I felt most amazingly fresh right to the end. He had taken it every night.

We began to hunt about for a village, and for some time failed to find one, a thick fog having

COLD, HUNGRY AND HAPPY.

Two 'drunken sailors' at Rostock.

Kriegsministerium.

Nr K 123 I/17 Berlin, den ....

Abteilung.

An
den Herrn Kommandant
Offiziersgefangenenlager
Magdeburg

Der Leutnant d. Res. Marschall hat den Befehl, sich zum Kriegsgefangenenlager in Magdeburg zu begeben, u. den englischen Hauptmann Cartwright von dort aus ins Gefangenenlager in Blankenburg zu transportieren.

Nachstehend ist die Photographie des Leutnant d. Res. Marschall.

Friedrich

INSPEKTION
DES
KRIEGSGEFANGENENLAGERS
BERLIN.

Magdeburg 26.1.17

Der Leutnant der Res. Marschall hat die Erlaubnis, mit einem englischen Offizier das Lagertor zu passieren.

Leut. u. Adjt.

Königlich Kommandantur
MAGDEBURG.

THE FORGED PASS.

Making the best of a bad job.

The Gleam of his petrol lighter revealed us.

In the very small hours.

Dodging the Sentry.

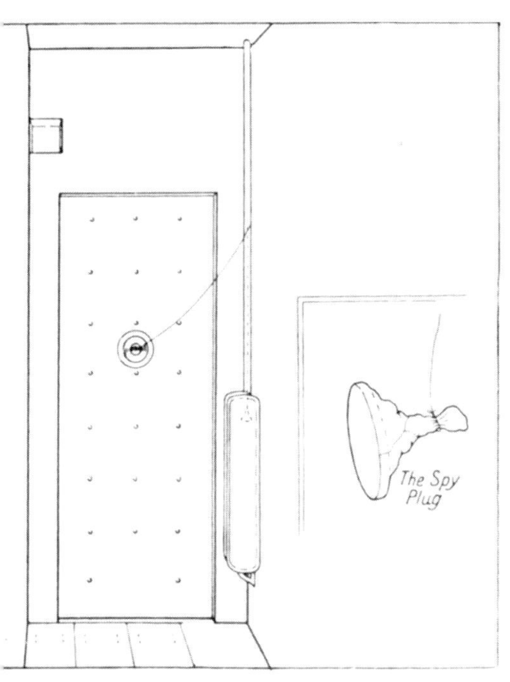

The Spy Plug—inside Cell No. 20.

What the General Saw.

Four free men: Lt. Templer, Lt. Insall, Capt. Harrison and Lt. Knight (seated). A photograph taken in the quarantine camp at Enschede, Holland, a few days after the escape. Templer is wearing clothes bought in Holland, and the others the clothes in which they escaped. Harrison is in his Guards officer's coat used in three different attempts. On Templer and Harrison may also be seen the ladies' blouses bought at Coevorden.

Captain Cartwright. A photograph taken by the Dutch police on his arrival in Holland.

come down when the wind dropped just after dawn. When we eventually found a small hamlet we approached an old woman who was just opening up her cottage, and Marshall asked her if she understood German.

Her reply was disconcerting, for with a horrible leer she put her finger to her mouth and whispered: 'Oh, it's like that, is it; you think you're in Holland!' adding quickly: 'This place is full of soldiers!'

Marshall darted off round the cottage and into a narrow lane, with me close on his heels—into the arms of the night sentries, who were just coming off duty, and that was the end of my second attempt.

Every one who knows anything of Germany invariably asks me why we bolted instead of bribing the old woman. The answer is that the whole thing happened much too quickly. Five seconds after the old woman had finished her horrid whisper we were almost literally in the arms of the Germans. Actually Marshall carried our whole supply of money to be used in just such an eventuality as this. Had he had thirty seconds in which to consider the situation he would have come back and offered the old woman a suitable present, which I have no doubt she would have accepted. She had spotted us on the instant as fugitives of some sort, and her every word and gesture had been an invitation. The shock of learning that we were still in Germany—after discussing the meal which we would order as soon as we reached civilisation—had thrown Marshall momentarily off his balance, and unfortunately the few seconds necessary for recovery were not available.

The hamlet—part of New Süstrum—is actually on the frontier line and we had walked into it from the WEST! On examining the compass later we found that some water had got into it when I fell into the drain, and this had frozen all round the edge of the card so that, although it would swing a little, just enough to make one think in the dark that it was free, it would settle down at almost any point in the circle. We must have wandered about right on the frontier, probably crossing and re-crossing it, for several hours.

We were taken to Meppen and dumped in the civil prison to await an escort for Magdeburg. The prison is on the west bank of the Emms, and we were guarded there by one very old warder who drank copiously of the claret which he was kind enough to buy and brew into 'punsch' for us, and for which we sent him out every fifteen or twenty minutes as long as he was fit for the job. The cell was on the ground floor and the window gave straight on to a garden with only a six-foot wall to it, so that there was only one old man, and he more than a little drunk, and one iron bar between us and the frontier. The only other occupants of the prison appeared to be one young deserter and the old warder's wife—an old witch of horrible aspect but quite deaf. But drunk as he was the old man kept his wits enough to lock the door after him, and we hadn't so much as a pocket-knife with which to cut the bar.

On the first of February 1917 we were taken back to Magdeburg and locked up in the police prison, where we arrived at midnight and where I had the satisfaction of finding my old friend Harrison, fit and full of plans, and the others of his party whose story has already been told.

The Germans tried all the usual tricks in the next few months to discover from Marshall and me how we had got out of the camp. They never had the vaguest idea how we did it or when, for dummies, which had been put in our beds after we left by good friends in the camp, had passed the 10 p.m. inspection and we were not missed until the 9 a.m. roll-call next morning.

Marshall was moved from Magdeburg four or five months later, and, after short periods in several different camps, eventually drifted back to the Scharnhorst again, where he repeated exactly the same exit and got clear away to Switzerland with another Frenchman.

Although the Germans were so sure of themselves at Magdeburg Prison that they did not even bother to take my civilian clothing away from me, I found when I arrived there that Harrison had already hatched a new scheme of which he will tell in the next chapter.

Shortly after my arrival at the prison I acquired, from home, a new luminous compass and a set of maps, and I will therefore put in here a note on the subject of stores and how we received them from home.

The supply of ' necessaries ' by friends at home began early in 1916. I cannot remember exactly how the first request for such things was communicated to them, but I believe it was contained in the letter which Harrison sent through a Frenchman and which he has described in Chapter III. His letter was sent to his sister, who communicated with my wife (then my fiancée), who kept me supplied thereafter with all I needed. Harrison and I had of course mentioned openly in our letters the bare fact that we had tried to escape and had been recaptured.

The ice once broken, we communicated with our friends in many ways. Numerous methods of hiding cypher messages in ordinary letters were used, each one introduced by a message of instruction hidden somehow in a parcel from home. They were difficult to work, and with the best of them it was only possible to embody a very short cypher message in a whole letter, and the sense of the letter had to be sacrificed to the necessity of so wording it as to bring in their right order the groups of letters forming the cypher. I never used them, though towards the end of my time I received a few short messages from Fox's friends (explained later). The censors knew enough to examine letters or books for pricked messages.

Many messages were exchanged for a time by

means of invisible writing. Several everyday liquids, such as lemon-juice, spittle, or, on certain kinds of paper, plain water, make a quite good invisible ink which can be developed by heat. After the escape of the Belgian, Terlinden, who gave my friends a lot of useful information when he reached London, I was provided with a good chemical ink and its developer, but by that time the Germans had tumbled to the game, and all letters—at least all those addressed to bad characters—were washed with half a dozen different liquids and vapours before delivery, and I could not risk using my ink. I only tried once with one of the early, simple inks, and the difficulty then was to explain to the recipient that the letter might prove more interesting if it were cooked. In one letter I drew some sort of silly picture which included a rabbit over which was written the invisible message. In the next letter (we wrote once a week or fortnight according to the rules for the time being of the particular camp we were in) I wrote, as if replying to some yarn which had been written to me; 'It was splendid getting the rabbit; I hope you cooked it.' The message was understood and the rabbit was heated, but with only partial success.

I much preferred to hide my messages in what appeared to be quite ordinary sentences, the real meaning of which could be puzzled out by the recipient but was most unlikely to penetrate the brains of the ex-waiters in the censors' office. Two examples will explain.

My wife had sent me a very good luminous compass and, after an attempted escape, the Germans had managed to annex it. I wanted another, but could do with one of less superior quality which must, however, be luminous; I wrote: 'I have lost the dear little copy of "Lead, Kindly Light" which you sent me. I should so like to have another, but the one which you sent was much too good considering how easily such small volumes get lost, but I did love the illuminated capitals.' The censor may have thought me a bit sloppy, but the compass came by return of post.

Again, I wanted maps of the Dutch frontier. I wrote: 'I know young Ambrose (which is *not* my name) better than you, and I know you've hit on the very thing he wants . . . If you want to please him, send him some of those pictures of the edge of the dear old cheese country.' By return of post came a complete set of motoring maps, covering the whole frontier and most of Germany, obtained with great difficulty through the R.A.C. I have the actual post card on which this message was sent before me as I write. It is crowded with small writing from top to bottom and every sentence contains a hidden meaning and refers to various efforts to establish communication by other means, and I cannot now imagine how the censors could fail to see that there was more in it than met the eye.

We used this kind of message continually and with complete success.

By the same method portable food (quite early in 1916 the Germans tumbled to the possibilities of beef lozenges, malted milk tablets, etc., and these were seized by the censors if they were sent openly), German money, small articles of civilian clothing such as felt hats, caps, collars, etc., wire-cutters, electric torches, hacksaw blades, etc., were asked for and sent. My wife sent me a supply of grey flannel —for home dyeing and tailoring—made up into an impossible pyjama suit of gigantic proportions. The Hun thought it was lovely. She also made up a length of cloth into a rug, which the censors passed without a qualm.

Though I obtained my compasses from home when I wanted them, I have seen quite useful ones made by British officers. The needles were somehow magnetized with the help of the camp electric current and were cunningly suspended on cotton. The luminous paint for the needles and points was picked off the dials of cheap German watches.

When parcels began to arrive from home the German saw quite soon the possibilities of the preserved food tin. He therefore decreed that the contents of all tins were to be decanted on to plates by the parcels censors before being handed to the owners. This was annoying of him, because the best way of hiding forbidden articles was to seal them in a tin of bully beef or sardines. The same rule was applied to boxes, packets, bottles, etc., and paper wrappings of all kind. Clothing and boots were handed over to tailors and shoemakers for examination. Books were given to one of the ex-waiter censors for examination. In Prussian camps these rules were very rigidly enforced. When parcels arrived they were opened by special parcels censors—who were often customs officers by trade—in the presence of the owners, at a counter in a special store-room in which were long ranges of pigeon-holes, one for each prisoner. Anything which the prisoner wanted for immediate consumption was decanted on the spot, the rest being pigeon-holed for another day. At a fixed hour daily the parcels room was opened and the food for the day decanted for those who asked for it. Anything made of paper, such as drawing or writing materials, was taken away for special examination. I have seen a censor sitting in the *Kommandantur* solemnly holding up to the light each separate sheet of a packet of Bromo. They had tried simply destroying the packets on sight, but the outcry had been so terrific and the appeals to neutral missions so many and plaintive that they had fallen back on the slower method.

In spite of these precautions they found very little to interest them, and the only loss I ever suffered was some German money which my wife had obtained with great difficulty and concealed in the stiffening of a sketch-block. I was in Magdeburg Jail at the time, but the glad news had not reached home when the parcel was sent. The censor there simply pulled the block to bits directly his eye lit on it. Of course I wrote a letter at once saying that it was quite impossible to defeat the censorship and how foolish it was to try to send hidden articles. I had not asked for them and they only got me into trouble—in fact, I was quite peevish about it—but I managed to convey in the same letter that the meat-tin business was still as safe as ever. For a long time after that the censors treated my parcels with a good deal of suspicion and were very careful not to let me have anything which had not been decanted and carefully raked through, but, since we could unlock the parcels room whenever they gave us five minutes' leisure (as will appear later), it didn't matter very much to us, and it made them feel real good.

At Magdeburg (Wagenhaus) for a time one of the censors used to cut cakes of soap in half to see what was in them, until one day a prisoner showed him how to hold a cake up to the light and see thereby that there was no deception. This interesting experiment was carried out with a tablet of Pears' transparent soap, but thereafter the intelligent fellow solemnly held all kinds of soap to the light and never cut another cake.

How the tins, packets, etc., in which forbidden articles were hidden, were got away uncensored after being pigeon-holed will appear presently, but I think the following trick deserves full marks. A British officer noticed that the parcels censor for the time being was a Hebrew, and he further discovered somehow that he was of the strictly orthodox persuasion. He therefore instructed his friends to send him a large cooked ham (which was certain to arrive rather past its prime but that could not be helped) with some maps and a wad of notes concealed in a cavity in its midst. The ham arrived when the Jew was, fortunately, on duty. He undid the outer covering, sniffed—he was nearly blind—and recoiled in horror. Having recovered enough to part the remaining wrappings with a knife, he begged its owner to take the horrid thing away with the remark: '*Bitte, Herr Hauptmann, kveek, nicht koscher, I am a Chew.*'

My wife went to an immense amount of trouble to persuade a Taunton grocer to obtain from a number of firms the paper labels with which their tins were wrapped. She used then very carefully to cut a tin in half, take out the beef, beans, cocoa or whatever it contained, wash it out and pack in the forbidden articles with ballast to make up the necessary weight. She would then get a tinsmith to solder the tin together again and would seal it up with one of the spare labels. The finished article looked and felt exactly like the original unopened tin.

Before any article containing forbidden goods was included in a parcel from home a letter was always sent indicating somehow the articles which must not be allowed to be censored. For instance, the letter would say: 'In the parcel I have sent off to-day is a tin of Allenbury's food which dear Aunt Enameline thought would be so good for you.' When the parcel came the tin—conspicuously labelled 'With love from Aunt Enameline'—would be refused for the day and pigeon-holed. The method was capable of so much variation as to be usable indefinitely.

We got the articles, uncensored, from the pigeon-holes by the following methods:

(i) By pocketing them from the counter when the censor had fetched some dozens from the pigeon-holes and was preparing, with watering mouth, to decant them. Sometimes we were allowed to go in with a censor and select what we wanted, when the pocketing was even easier. The censors were always nearly blind, otherwise they would have been *Kanonenfutter* instead of censors. The only trouble was that there were always a lot of idle Huns hanging hungrily about the parcels room in the hope of picking up scraps, and they made things rather difficult.

(ii) By handing a small tin of food or an empty sardine tin with some oil sticking to it to the censor, as a token of disinterested affection, with one hand, while pocketing the selected articles with the other. For this game one had to know the censor, and be sure of him, and it could only be done when no other German was in sight. Generally it was best to announce a birthday and persuade a censor to take one alone, at an unusual hour, into the parcels room.

(iii) By opening the parcels room with a prisoner-made key during the night; or making a private entrance through the floor, roof or wall—the room was generally made by boarding off part of a corridor or large room, the few small rooms existing in the old factories or warehouses, in which prisoners were generally kept, being taken for offices. In several camps entry by one means or the other was quite easy. There were skilled locksmiths and burglars in every camp. At Küstrin[1] we had unrestricted access to the parcels room all night. When a hole was discovered we said it must be our Russian allies (the type of Russian at Küstrin is described later) stealing food, and the Germans believed us. I don't think they ever knew, in any camp, that we did our own censoring except when Hardy and I gave up the keys at Küstrin. We had the censors so well trained by that time that we had no need to break into the parcels room, though we knew we could still do it if we wanted to. In some camps the situation of the parcels room made both the last two methods described above quite impossible.

It happened once that the Germans at Küstrin discovered, in an underground corridor, an iron grating which had been partly sawn through. The Commandant knew that escape that way was impossible and contented himself with tying to the grating a label bearing the one word *Zwecklos* (useless) with his signature and official stamp. There came a time when the parcels room was to be turned into an office, and a new room was made.

[1] See Chapter VII.

On the last night before the change over Hardy and I unlocked the door of the old parcels room with our own keys, made by Hardy out of old nails and sardine-tin openers bound together with bits of wire—there were two locks—tied the keys to the hanging lamp with a label bearing the one word *Zwecklos* and the perfectly good signature and official stamp of the Commandant, and locked the door again with the snap padlock.

Twice I received parcels containing forbidden stores without having had any warning letter, and it was only by the greatest luck that I was not caught out. The first time was at Magdeburg. A parcel was opened for me and was found to contain a seven-pound tin of biscuits. Knowing the rules, I went to my room for an empty tin of the same size. When I returned I found a big crowd in the room and my tin sitting invitingly on one end of the counter. Without any particular object, except to hurry the censor, I banged down the empty tin, picked up the full one, and walked away with it. I expected to be cursed and called back at once, but the censor, who was fully occupied, never noticed me at all, and, unhindered, I carried the tin to my room. When, after a week or two, I got to the end of the biscuits, I was astonished to find a beautifully made double bottom containing a valuable outfit of maps. My wife had been to immense trouble to obtain the paper cover of the tin with which she had sealed it up like a new one after a tinsmith had soldered the maps into the bottom. Her warning letter had been much delayed and arrived days after I had discovered the maps.

The second time was at Küstrin, and the parcel was sent by some friends of Fox, an officer in the Scots Guards who had escaped some time before and had made very thorough arrangements for the supply of necessaries to certain prisoners who were known to be trying to escape. I was the only Englishman in the camp and was on good terms with all the censors. It was an ordinary-looking parcel from, apparently, Fortnum & Mason, or some such firm whose parcels always contained good food but little else to interest the censors. Anyhow, I did not suspect the parcel and said I would take everything on the spot. There was no one else in the room, and the censor, from sheer laziness, pushed the whole lot at me and locked up. The parcel was simply stuffed with maps, compasses, electric torches and information about frontiers, and included the bottle of prunes which I shall mention later. The letter warning me that a parcel containing contraband had been sent off arrived the next day.

Fox's friends began to operate towards the end of 1917 or beginning of 1918, and it was quite evident that they were in touch with our families and were thoroughly well informed in all matters of interest to escaping prisoners. I think that the first I heard of them was in a letter from one of them giving me the cypher in which they would communicate. The fact that the letter was from a stranger, and extraordinarily uninteresting, was quite enough to make me study it carefully and worry out its hidden meaning.

In order to avoid the spreading of the damage in case of discovery these parcels were sent only to one officer in each of three or four different camps, but they contained enough stores for each of those officers to equip several others. They sent very small but quite serviceable luminous compasses and very small electric torches, both of which could be hidden much more easily than the ordinary varieties, and maps of Germany covering the country from wherever the recipients might be to the Dutch and Swiss frontiers.

They sent also valuable information about the frontiers, how they were guarded, what roads were patrolled, where the frontier zones (in which all movement was controlled by special regulations) began, and the actual disposition of the sentries in certain areas. They sent me also the identity card to which I shall refer in my chapter about Schweidnitz. This was an excellent forgery of a workman's card, but it had, as a matter of fact, one fault which would probably escape the notice of any detective or gendarme although it was at once apparent to the eye of the practised amateur of forgery. The circular rubber stamp used was that of the 'Polizeidirektion' of Wurttemberg, or some other non-Prussian town, but it had in its midst an Imperial bird of the breed only raised in Prussia. An old photograph of myself furnished by my wife had been faked and reproduced with a neat neck-rag in place of the more usual collar and tie. As it happened, I never had an opportunity of using it. It was the escaped 'manaic,' Hardy, who gave them all the information necessary to the manufacture of this masterpiece and persuaded them to have it made and sent to me, and I shall never cease to regret that I had no opportunity of testing its powers. They also sent me clear instructions indicating how and where help might be found within the frontiers of Germany, but I was in Zorndorf at the time and, as appears later, escape from that fortress was to all ordinary mortals impossible.

One scrap of information which they sent me came in a parcel containing the usual assortment of tins and a bottle of dried prunes. The warning letter which, as I have described, arrived after the parcel, indicated some of the tins and the bottle of prunes. The tins contained some maps, etc., and were easily dealt with. I don't remember what made me suspect the prunes, but I took them all out of the bottle and found nothing, so began to eat them. Half-way through them I bit on one whose stone seemed less hard than the rest and spat it out, thinking it was rotten. On second thoughts I picked up the stone and examined it. It had been cracked, the kernel had been removed and a small piece of tissue paper, covered with minute writing and wrapped tightly in a bit of oil-silk, had been inserted in its place.

Unfortunately, all these parcels came to me in

Küstrin when I was the only British officer there, so I was quite unable to distribute the surplus stores and was obliged to hide them all in my baggage—with the exception of one compass, which I gave to a Russian colonel of the old régime (the same that Harrison has mentioned in his Torgau chapter). He was well prepared, spoke German fairly well, and the last I heard of him was that he had disappeared from the train on his way from Küstrin to another camp.

V

MAGDEBURG PRISON

By M. C. C. HARRISON

In the civil prison at Magdeburg—Possibilities for escape—Obtaining a skeleton key—The parcels office—Cartwright's arrival—A ruined opportunity of escape—Clothes for a daylight escape—A 'spy-hole' picture—Dyeing a coat—Moving cells—Escape with Cartwright from the prison—A two hundred miles' walk—Recapture—Return to Magdeburg—My courts martial—Collecting contraband stores—A last effort with the key.

AT 8.30 p.m. on the 14th December 1916 the party of five English and seven Russian officers, who had been moved from Torgau, arrived in the civil prison at Magdeburg. The early prospect of food and a night's rest revived our spirits to a certain extent. Our arrival in the prison seemed to cause a commotion. I suppose I must have been doing my share of talking, for my earliest recollection of the place is a familiar voice shouting from inside one of the cells: 'Is that you, Harrison?' It was my old friend Templer. I was extremely cheered at the thought of meeting him once more. As events turned out, I had few opportunities of having any conversation with him. He was only doing a short term of rigorous imprisonment, during which time he was not allowed out of his cell for any purpose whatsoever. He had just completed a year's imprisonment at Wesel.

We were ushered along the passage into the office, where, in accordance with the usual custom, we were searched before being hustled off to our respective cells.

The prison, designed for remand and short sentence prisoners, is part of a large building, which comprises the municipal offices, head police station, and courts of justice. It is built round a courtyard, and fronts on a main street near the centre of the town. Each cell contained a stool, a jug and basin, and a bed consisting of three planks hinged and locked to the wall throughout the day. The locks, however, did not worry us much, and eventually the warders had to abandon the task of trying to enforce the Commandant's order that beds were to be kept chained to the wall throughout the day. Instructions posted in the corridor directed that these small cells be used only for 'drunks' and for not more than forty-eight hours by any one prisoner. I was more than seven months in mine. The cells in the stories immediately above and below our corridor were used for German civilians, the upper ones being reserved for women. For the benefit of Neutral Missions, who might have questioned why we were kept in a civil prison, each cell was labelled 'OFFIZIERARRESTZELLE,' and a large piece of cardboard was nailed in the corridor of our flat also, bearing the inscription : 'KRIEGSGARNISONARRESTANSTALT.'

My cell, No. 20 (see page 192), was one of the smallest in the prison and measured three feet four inches by ten feet six. If I stood in the centre, hands on hips, my elbows touched the two side walls. The bed bugs were so plentiful that I managed in the first week to get permission to visit the Camp Commandant to show him the swollen state of my arms and legs. Captain Kunz, who was in charge of the prison, had previously announced his inability to improve matters. His invariable reply to all our requests and complaints was: 'I can do nothing; I am not Commandant.'

To my request to have the prison disinfected the Commandant replied: 'If you are not prepared to put up with conditions as you find them, you should not have let yourself be taken prisoner.' I thought at the time that this came well from a man who had been no nearer than Magdeburg to any front. I then told him that the other prisons in which I had been were kept in a more sanitary condition. He replied: 'Oh, you have been in other prisons, have you? Well that proves that you are no gentleman,' and I was promptly kicked out of the office.

We now had a fair idea of the type of man with whom we had to deal—the very worst kind of bullying Prussian.

If my readers will bear in mind the unpleasant character of these two senior officers they will, I think, find it easier to make allowances for the apparently childish ruses we had subsequently to adopt to achieve our ends.

I do not want to give the impression that all the Germans who looked after us here were fools, but our only hope was to concentrate on those that were.

In addition to the warders, a military guard was found and changed daily in the ordinary way. They lived in a room at the end of our passage and furnished a sentry for duty in the corridor outside our locked doors day and night.

How were we going to get out of this place ?

There was no question of going through the floor or ceiling. There were occupied cells both above and below. The cell windows were only a foot square, strongly barred, and placed at the top of the outer wall. The windows overlooked a court-yard entirely surrounded by buildings and guarded by an extra sentry at night. Having read Captain Hardy's account of his escape from Halle, and knowing that it is not exaggerated, I will not say that it would have been impossible to go this way, but it seemed so to me at the time.

There remained the doors. In order to ventilate the cells, doors were opened daily from 7.30 to 8.30 p.m. Prisoners were not allowed to leave their cells during this hour, but guards were fre-quently slack in enforcing the order. We soon discovered that the sentry whose job it was to open our doors used the same key for all cells, for the office door and for the one at the end of the passage, through which we had entered on first arrival and which I will call 'Door X.' I used to spend most of the ventilating hour practising picking the lock of my own cell door. If I could become proficient at this, and bide my time for a suitable type of sentry, I felt quite confident that an escape could be made through the door X into the municipal buildings. To get out of them into the street there would be just one more door to negotiate at the foot of the stairs. It was a large double door, wide enough to take a 'Black Maria,' and did not appear to be a very formidable obstacle.

For picking the lock of my cell door I used two sardine-tin openers each bent into the shape of an L. The locks were new and stiff and of a modern design, and for a time I experienced considerable difficulty. The spring was not difficult to locate and lift with one hook, but the catch in the bolt did not always stop in the same place, and it often took me a long time to find it with the other hook. This annoyed me very much, as I could only hope to succeed by training myself to open door X with lightning rapidity. Try as I would I could not make sure of a quick job. We had, however, a workable means of getting out of the prison. Campbell and Graham-Toler were for coming with me, but none of us were anything like properly 'mobilised' for a winter journey.

The difficulty of collecting and keeping 'mobilisation stores' while in prison was very often much harder than the actual escape.

By arranging diversions for the sentry during the evening airing hour we were able to pick the lock of the office door and get at our parcels which were kept there.

Early in January, a British officer, interned in Magdeburg Camp, was sent to our prison for five days for failing to salute a German officer. From him we learnt that officers in prison who required dental treatment were brought to the camp for the purpose. He also told me that Templer was in that camp.

The next day, according to a prearranged plan, when returning from exercise in the courtyard, an Englishman and a Russian started bickering and almost came to blows in our corridor. I shoved them both into the nearest cell, and, slamming the door, shouted to the sentry for the key. He, thoroughly entering into the spirit of the joke, promptly handed it to me. Hastily taking an impression of it on a wad of oxo cubes which I held in my left hand, I locked the door and went on to my cell, leaving the sentry to release the brawlers.

Once in my cell I made a drawing of the key and wrote a note to Templer, asking him to try and get a skeleton key made in the camp.

That evening I developed violent toothache, and so appalling was my agony that I was promised a visit to the dentist the very next day.

As I expected, Templer was one of the first to greet me on my arrival in the camp. In a language which my escort would not understand I managed to say to him : 'I have a note for you ; follow me,' before I was told to keep my mouth shut. While I was being marched up the stairs to the dentist's room I dropped the note containing the drawing of the key, and had the satisfaction of seeing Templer place his foot on it.

About twenty minutes later, while the dentist was grinding away at a perfectly good tooth,

I heard a loud and heated discussion break out in the next room, and amongst many voices easily recognised that of Templer. So well did he play his part that I doubt if even the other Englishmen realised that he was conveying to the patient in the dentist's chair next door that the key would be ready the following Wednesday and exactly where he would find it, so that he could grab it in passing and slip it into his pocket.

Determined to waste no time, I had toothache again on the following Tuesday and was warned for the dentist on the Wednesday. So far everything seemed to be going splendidly.

Imagine my dismay when Wednesday came and I was marched, not to the camp, but to a dentist in the town, the camp dentist having been sent to the front. Almost every day I agitated for another visit to the dentist, believing that a new man would be appointed to work in the camp. Although I must have had a hole bored in every tooth in my head, I never saw the camp again.

Friends of Templer's in the camp, all of them unknown to me, had made a key out of a part of an iron bedstead, and were very agitated because I could no longer come and fetch it as arranged. Templer himself had been moved elsewhere shortly after my visit to the camp, and the others, all foreigners, realising that I could not get to the camp, decided that they would have to send the key to me. One of their number therefore put the key inside his boot, went to the Commandant's office with some utterly frivolous complaint and refused to leave until he was marched straight off to the prison, where, that same evening, he handed the key over to me.

The key was a complete success and we soon found that, with careful manipulation, all doors could be opened and re-locked reasonably quickly. Our chances of effecting a successful escape were now

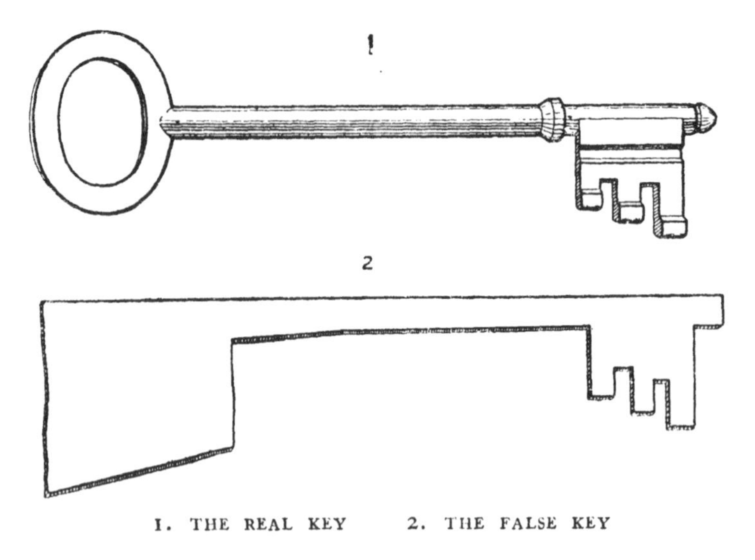

1. THE REAL KEY 2. THE FALSE KEY

materially increased. We hid the key in a ventilator in the passage.

Could anyone be served better by his greatest friends than I was by these stout-hearted allies whom I had never met ?

From now on, almost daily, the key was used to let some one into the office during the evening airing hour. At least one of our number would spend most of the hour, locked up inside, either getting at our parcels or hiding mobilisation stores in there.

On one of these occasions we must have moved

something sufficiently to arouse our jailer's suspicion, for he suddenly elected to padlock the door, as well as bolt and lock it when he left for the night.

I soon became proficient at picking this padlock, but in re-locking it one night I was rather hustled through the sentry not taking the usual interest in the diversion arranged for his benefit. The result was that I only half locked it and the jailer could not open it in the morning with his key. To get into the office he had to break the padlock.

He was furious with the guard and was quite certain they had tried to get in there during the night to loot our parcels.

When he had recovered his temper, curiously enough, he came to me for sympathy, bringing the broken padlock with him. He told me exactly how much he himself had paid for it in order to guard against dishonest sentries looting our parcels at night, and now they had gone and broken his lock and his money had been wasted. I was most sympathetic and eventually made him a present of one of the many padlocks I had bought in order to study the art of picking locks. It was a powerful-looking padlock, and he was extremely grateful. Of course I kept one of the keys for my own use.

Careful organisation and close co-operation between those actually making an attempt and their accomplices was always essential, and for the scheme which we now contemplated it was necessary to make the most minute arrangement with some of the other prisoners.

This could not be done satisfactorily during the exercise hour, the only occasion on which we were, officially, allowed to forgather. But, fortunately, human nature being what it is, even in a German prison, there existed a necessity which the severest Prussian discipline could not altogether suppress, and this gave an opening for other less formal meetings.

One of the larger cells had been fitted out as a lavatory, with ample accommodation, on the 'sociable' principle, for some half dozen visitors, but to which the sentry had orders to admit not more than three at a time.

As a conspirators' rendezvous it had many good points, but these were more than neutralised by the fact that it was quite unheated. To justify anything like a prolonged session the conspirators had to expose themselves to the icy temperature of a concrete cell with a broken window, where the thermometer stood at −20 degrees Centigrade.

The place was, however, very badly lighted, and some genius hit upon the plan of pinning to his trousers a piece of pink paper which, with a coat suitably draped around it and in the semi-darkness of the cell, gave to an inquisitive or impatient sentry the necessary impression of bare flesh. Only by the aid of this little device were we able to hold our meetings in that arctic cell with no very great discomfort.

Fearing that we might be moved to another prison at any moment, we decided to go ahead with our plan and break out at the first opportunity, instead of waiting for milder weather, as we should have much preferred to do.

On the 1st February 1917 arrangements were well ahead, when who should arrive in the prison but my old friend Cartwright.

Imagine my surprise. I had never expected to see him again in Germany in view of the determination of the authorities to separate us.

Of course he simply had to come with us, and as soon as I had explained the situation to him he was all for it. He was very keen that Marshall, who had come to prison with him, should join us. The latter officer's knowledge of the language would make it possible for us to use the train, and though we had previously decided to walk to the Dutch frontier, Cartwright was not optimistic of a long winter trek. Finally, it was arranged that Marshall should come with Cartwright and me, shepherding us at least part of the way by train, and that Campbell and Graham-Toler should try to walk all the way.

So safe did the Germans imagine the prison to be that they did not even bother to take away Cartwright's and Marshall's civilian clothes. Now that we had decided to go by train, I had to collect better garments, which was not very easy in a prison. A socialist German orderly rose to the occasion and produced some white collars made of paper, which we persuaded him were normally worn with uniform. The appearance of my other garments, all converted uniform, was considerably improved by a little more amateur tailoring.

By the end of February we were all ready when Campbell, Graham-Toler and myself received a notification that our appeal against the sentence for mutiny at Torgau would be heard on Monday, 5th March 1917. Not knowing what might happen to us after that, we decided not to wait for it. We selected 4th March, as being a Sunday, and therefore the quietest day in the public offices through which we should have to pass. We ascertained that the door into the street from the municipal building was left open daily until 9 p.m., at which hour it was locked for the night.

At 8 p.m., during the ventilating hour on 4th March, Campbell, Graham-Toler, Marshall, Cartwright and myself were collected in cell No. 30 (see page 192). We wore military great-coats over our civilian clothes and our rucksacks were stored under the bed. The sentry and the under-officer in charge of the guard were in the main corridor C. The rest of the guard were in the guard-room, at the farther end of the corridor. Two prisoners started a scrap in the corridor B. The sentry and the under-officer turned into that corridor to get a better view. I opened the door X and passed through with Marshall and Cartwright. One of the other two locked the door after us. They were to give us five minutes to get clear of the building before following. After their departure the door would be locked by another prisoner and the key returned to its recognised hiding-place in the passage, where with luck it would survive the inevitable search and perhaps be of use to some other prisoner at a later date.

Arrived at the foot of the stairs, we found the large door into the street securely bolted and locked. A hasty reconnaisance revealed no other exit. Graham-Toler and Campbell arrived to find us trying to force the bolt, which our united strength failed to move an inch. A few minutes later a terrific eruption of bellowing from above told us that we had been missed. We hastily sought what cover we could in the basement, hoping to be able to get out when the gates were opened in the morning or perhaps after the storm had subsided that night.

We survived the first hasty search of the building, but our jailer arrived on the scene of action about half an hour later and organised a further hunt. The policeman who was sent down to the basement shouted from the very cellar in which we were hiding: 'There is no one here.' Unfortunately he stopped to light a cigar, and the gleam of his petrol lighter revealed us all huddled together in one corner. He was quite calm and collected about it and led us quietly back to the prison. Here we were received by our own jailer, who was anything but calm and collected, and gave a most perfect exhibition of Prussian fury. He seized the sentry's loaded rifle, had us jammed together at one end of the corridor and announced that he was going to shoot us. Marshall told him he had no right to do so, to which he replied : ' I have the right, and I am going to shoot you all.'

I am quite convinced that he meant to kill at least one of us, but in order to make a certainty of hitting some one he came so close to us that Campbell managed to throw the muzzle of the rifle up over our heads just as he was going to fire.

A general mix-up followed, in which the guard joined, and so great was the noise that the civil police came in to see what was happening. They soon got the situation in hand and we were locked up in our cells. Practically everything we had was taken away and put into the office to be kept for the Commandant's inspection.

Subsequently we discovered that had we made our attempt on any week-day we would probably have succeeded, as it was only on Sundays that the ' Black Maria ' gate was locked at 6 p.m. instead of 9 p.m.

A glorious opportunity had been ruined.

Prisoners who had been recaptured at a frontier always commanded more sympathy than those caught in the act of breaking out. Personally I always felt more flattened out and discouraged in the latter case. Caught at a frontier, one had at least had a run for one's money, and had almost certainly gained information and experience which would be of the greatest value in subsequent attempts. On the other hand, if the actual break-out failed, apart from the danger of being shot in the attempt, weeks, perhaps months, of difficult preparation were wasted and all one's carefully collected ' mobilisation stores ' were lost to the Germans at a single stroke. So I always felt, and I can assure my readers that after this failure I felt more depressed than at any other time during my captivity.

The Appeal Court sat the next day and decided that our appeal was without foundation. We were told that our sentence of six months' imprisonment would start from that day, and that none of the seven months which we had already done would count. We were, however, given the option of having our case brought before the Supreme War Court in Berlin. Most of us were getting rather tired of prison life by now, and all except me decided to press their cases no further in the hope of being let out of prison in six months' time. I, on the other hand, had already been warned for trial on several other charges, and could see no prospect of ever being let out of prison, so had nothing to lose by an appearance before this Supreme Court.

Moreover, knowing that the skeleton key was still available for another effort, I had no desire to be sent away to a ' long-sentence ' in prison.

On my return to prison from the court I noticed the jailer was in a much better frame of mind, and, getting in touch with Cartwright, decided to have a shot at saving what we could from the wreck of our belongings, which were still in the office. On some pretext or other Cartwright and I managed to get in there at the same time, and we found the jailer in quite good form and prepared to joke about the whole business of our absurd attempt.

He was, however, firm that everything that he had taken off us must go to the Commandant for examination. In vain we picked up certain articles and tried to persuade him that it was useless to send them up for examination, but in spite of his obstinacy we managed between us to save a little. Our best coup was when Cartwright retrieved all his money, which he had left concealed in the shoulder-strap of his black military overcoat.

He had intended to use this garment as a civilian coat in the train and had left the shoulder-straps on till the last possible moment in the hopes that the garment, being military, would escape confiscation in the event of early recapture. Cartwright, pointing to the shoulder-straps, told the jailer it was a military overcoat and claimed the right to have it back, but the latter was firm and said that it was for the Commandant to decide. Pressing his point Cartwright said: 'But this coat is rotten,' as he pulled one shoulder-strap off. Still the jailer was obdurate, whereupon Cartwright repeated: 'But you can see it is absolutely rotten; it is no use sending it up'—and he pulled the other shoulder-strap off. We were then pushed out of the office, shoulder-straps, money and all.

The money at any rate was saved.

A few days later Cartwright persuaded the adjutant to return his overcoat owing to the extreme cold. It had been covered with the inevitable brass buttons, shoulder-straps and braid. My thermos flask containing a reserve compass, some metal files and some maps, hidden between the vacuum glass and outer case, was also returned.

Having saved the key and part, at least, of our mobilisation stores we had not done too badly.

During the ensuing weeks we were subjected to many searches by detectives from Berlin and Magdeburg. These experts confined their attention to the prisoners and the contents of their cells, giving no thought to the passage—where the key reposed—nor to the office, where most of our forbidden stores were hidden. We lost nothing of any importance.

Although the opening of the cell doors in the evening was discontinued after our attempt, sufficient opportunities occurred for gaining access to our stores in the office.

Finding no clue, the authorities came to the conclusion that we must have had outside assistance. A large block of metal was accordingly fixed over the keyhole on the outer side of the door X and two policemen were put on duty on the stairs every night.

After the storm had subsided, we reviewed the situation and came to the conclusion that every conceivable precaution had been taken to guard against an escape by night.

We therefore decided to go out by day.

Since a long walk through Magdeburg in daylight would have to be undertaken before reaching the open country, our clothes would have to be sufficiently presentable not to attract attention.

Cartwright's single-breasted (old pattern) private soldier's military overcoat was an obvious start, and in a short time he had made a good job of it. Apart from the gold buttons, badges of rank, etc., which were to be left on until the last moment, it would pass as an ordinary mufti overcoat. He got a pair of blue trousers with a large red stripe from a Belgian artillery officer in exchange for an old pair of his own. His overcoat being single-breasted necessitated some show of jacket beneath it. He cut a collar and pair of lapels from the seat of his trousers and fixed them on with string beneath his arms. The gap in his trousers was filled in with part of an old shirt.

The socialist orderly produced celluloid collars, but would have nothing to do with getting a hat. One was ultimately smuggled down from the camp for Cartwright by a French orderly who concealed it between two plates.

My invisible ink communication with home now bore fruit in the shape of a soft felt cricket hat, which arrived inside a pot of jam carefully wrapped up in oil-silk. It was absurdly limp, but by rubbing soap into it I stiffened it up and shaped it to look like a

Homburg hat and darkened it with blacking. I dyed the legs of my khaki trousers with ink.

My Guard's overcoat was always good for another trip, but I should have to take about eight inches off the length to make a civilian roll collar. As long as the brass buttons and badges of rank remained the alteration would arouse no suspicion. For the job I required at least a fortnight's undisturbed work, and this I could not hope for as long as the sentries were free to observe me through the spy-hole in the door.

If I placed an envelope over the spy-hole or blocked it with paper in any way, suspicion would at once be aroused.

I talked the matter over with Cartwright at exercise and between us we decided that the best way of averting suspicion would be to place a picture, calculated to appeal to the German mind, in my spy-hole.

At first we thought a picture of an eye would meet the case, then a miniature painting of the cell was debated, but finally we decided that Cartwright would paint, in water-colours, a picture such as a man might hope to see if he was of the type that peered through the keyholes of bedroom doors.

The next day Cartwright gave me a really fine masterpiece. He had paid so much attention to detail that it was obviously up to me to take steps to guard it against confiscation.

I melted some lead paper and stuck it on the back of the picture, and with a piece of cotton attached it to the vertical hot-water pipe in the corner of the cell. By carefully adjusting the length of thread I made the picture drop from its position in the spy-hole, on the door being opened, and automatically hide itself behind the radiator. A towel drying on the radiator broke the shock of the fall and insured complete silence. Practice brought perfection.

The 'hanging' of the picture aroused great excitement amongst the prison officials and camp Commandant's staff. Their early efforts to loot it were too ridiculous to narrate, but as no one suspected its real object I was able to get on with my work in comparative peace. The sentries soon contented themselves by nudging each other in the passage and treating it as a huge joke, possibly because they could see how infuriated were their own officers.

The picture continued to do its work splendidly for about a month, which gave me ample time to complete all preparations. As events turned out, it attracted a greater crowd and was the cause of more comment than expected. The most offensive visitor was a fat old German general, whose idea of inspecting a prison was to creep down the passage on tiptoe and peep through the spy-hole of all cell doors. When he got to my cell and saw the picture to say he was livid with rage would be putting it mildly. He had the door opened immediately and shouted at me for quite five minutes on end. It so happened I was having my breakfast at the far end of the cell, and when he had done shouting I asked him, as politely as I could in German, to what picture he referred. He immediately turned round

A GENERAL PEEPS THROUGH THE SPY-HOLE

towards the door, saying: 'Why this picture here of course.'

To his surprise he could see nothing. He had so completely lost control of himself that my efforts to soothe him by suggesting that he must have made some mistake, let his imagination get the better of him, or had seen it somewhere else, were of no avail. He left the cell obviously not satisfied.

I was now faced with the alternative of ' standing down ' for a week or so, or of ignoring the episode. After a consultation with Cartwright the latter course was selected as the wiser. The general was sure to visit the prison again, the picture was necessary to enable me to get on with my work, and there appeared to be nothing to be gained by suspending work. The general imagined the picture had been put there especially for his benefit. Well, as long as he thought it was there for no other motive so much the better.

As expected, he came round again the following morning at about the same hour when he had the door opened even quicker than the first time and shouted at me in a more furious tone, if possible. Up to now I had adopted an air of injured innocence but on this occasion I had placed a circular patch of white tooth-paste on the floor by the door and could not refrain from laughing straight in the general's face as he stooped down trying to pick up the tooth-paste thinking he had got the picture. What could he do ? I suppose I was already in the worst cell in Germany, waiting to start a sentence of six months ; I was also awaiting trial by court martial on several other charges. He instructed the jailer to get that picture at all costs.

In order to keep up the belief that the picture

was merely there as a practical joke it was necessary to play up to this theory to a certain degree. One day the jailer thought he had it. Seeing it in position from the outside, he opened the door like lightning and pounced on an envelope that I had stuck over the back of it. The picture had been in position underneath, but was by now automatically safe behind the radiator. Seizing the envelope he hastily pulled out the piece of pink lining paper from the inside, only to find that it was full of pepper, which flew all over his face. Detectives were called in, but still the picture survived.

Early in May the jailer came into my cell one day to inform me of the latest German victory, the probable end of the war and the early release of all prisoners except those who had sentences to complete. Fatigued by his own eloquence, he backed and leant against the radiator. His fingers came in contact with a piece of cotton, he pulled and there was the picture in his hand. I have seldom seen a man look so pleased. He shoved it in his pocket and rushed off to the Commandant, doubtless expecting to receive an Iron Cross.

In due course the alterations to the coat were completed, and as it was still covered with brass buttons and badges of rank, the new roll collar would pass unnoticed provided I wore the garment often enough.

I next had to make arrangements to have it dyed, since grey mufti overcoats were very uncommon.

Although there might be some in existence, the colour would have been sufficiently out of the ordinary to have been conspicuous. Though I had taken the greatest trouble to make every stitch look as if it had been done by machine, and also to press and iron it with my nail, I did not flatter myself that my tailoring was perfect.

Experimenting in my cell with a spare piece of cloth I found it could be dyed a very attractive chocolate colour with a solution of permanganate of potash ($KMNO_4$). I had been allowed some of these crystals as a disinfectant, and as my cell was known to be full of bed bugs, my excessively high demand did not cause special comment. As might be expected, I found, by experiment, that I could get many different shades of chocolate, up to a certain degree of darkness, when the cloth would not take more dye, and no matter how much stronger I made the solution the colour remained the same. This was most satisfactory, as the dyeing process would have to be carried out in my bath when time would be a very important factor.

The bath was in a separate cell on the floor below and each prisoner was locked into it once a week for twenty minutes. It was customary on these occasions to use overcoats for dressing-gowns, and in due course I was marched to the bath cell wearing my newly completed coat (always with brass buttons and badges of rank). Directly I was locked in the cell I let about six inches of water into the bath and then threw in a packet of permanganate crystals.

In my endeavour to make a certainty of having a sufficiently strong solution to ensure the garment being dyed the same shade all over, I suppose I must have thrown in about ten times as much permanganate as would have done the job. In a few seconds the coat was a perfect colour all over. I could not leave it long in the bath knowing the jailer would return in about ten minutes, and I required at least five to get the water out of the garment before he came. To my relief I found that only colourless water came out, so I presumed the result of this hasty dyeing process would not cause the coat to dry in patches of different shades of brown.

On removing the plug, to my horror I found I had also dyed the whole of the bottom of the bath. I hastily added some more water, as with my soaking overcoat my only chance now was to get back to my cell before any suspicion was aroused. Since its arrival in Germany my coat had had such rough use it is not surprising that the dirt from it made even this strong solution of permanganate look like genuine filthy water.

Presently the jailer arrived to tell me my time was up. I was all ready for him with my soaking coat on over my naked body. Directly he opened the door I ran upstairs back to my cell, hung the coat up in a corner and put on some other garments. The jailer, seeing that I had not emptied the bath proceeded to do so himself. It was not long before he was after me wanting to know 'what the hell

I had done to the bath ? ' I told him I had merely tried to disinfect myself against the vermin in the cell. Contrary to his usual custom he listened patiently to my explanation, but terminated the discussion with '*Das ist ein Schweinerei.*'

A few minutes later I heard him telling the under-officer of the guard that he was on his way to the Commandant to report 'The filthy habits of the English captain Harrison.'

A mild storm followed, terminating in my being ordered to pay for a whole new bath.

As the coat dried, my most optimistic hopes were more than realised. So perfect was the colour, Mr. Pullar might well have been proud had it been dyed at his works in Perth.

Having nowhere to hide it, I wore it on all possible occasions, which was the best way of averting suspicion.

By the 7th May mobilisation was complete. My cell (No. 20) was not conveniently situated for the contemplated scheme. Cell No. 28 (see plan), which would suit me much better, was empty.

How could I persuade the authorities to move me there ?

That night as I lay in bed I rubbed the edge of an old bottle against the wall in such a manner as to imitate the sound of a metal file at work. Presently the suspicions of the sentry were aroused, and I could hear the whole guard being warned. I repeated the filing noise at intervals, and suddenly my door was flung open by the under-officer in charge, who found me apparently fast asleep in bed. This was repeated two or three times during the night. The bars in my window were carefully examined the following day. The same performance was continued the next night with a new guard.

On the following day I was moved to cell No. 28.

The moving process is worth recording. It necessitated several journeys, the sentry always following me from one cell to the other with a loaded rifle at full cock pressed against the small of my back. On one of these trips the rifle went off by accident just as I was turning into my cell; the bullet missed me and went into the guard-room, where it caused much havoc but unfortunately hit no one.

The next day I was warned for trials by court martial on May 15th and May 18th. The former was for making a hole in the roof of my cell at Torgau, for which trial I had engaged counsel. The other was for 'insulting superior officers by placing an immoral picture in my cell door.'

Fearing I might be moved to a 'long-sentence' prison after these trials, we again decided not to wait for them.

Our mobilisation was complete and all that remained to be done was to school the necessary accomplices.

The under-officer in charge of the guard invariably sat at a table by the door of the guard-room, which enabled him to see the length of the corridor,

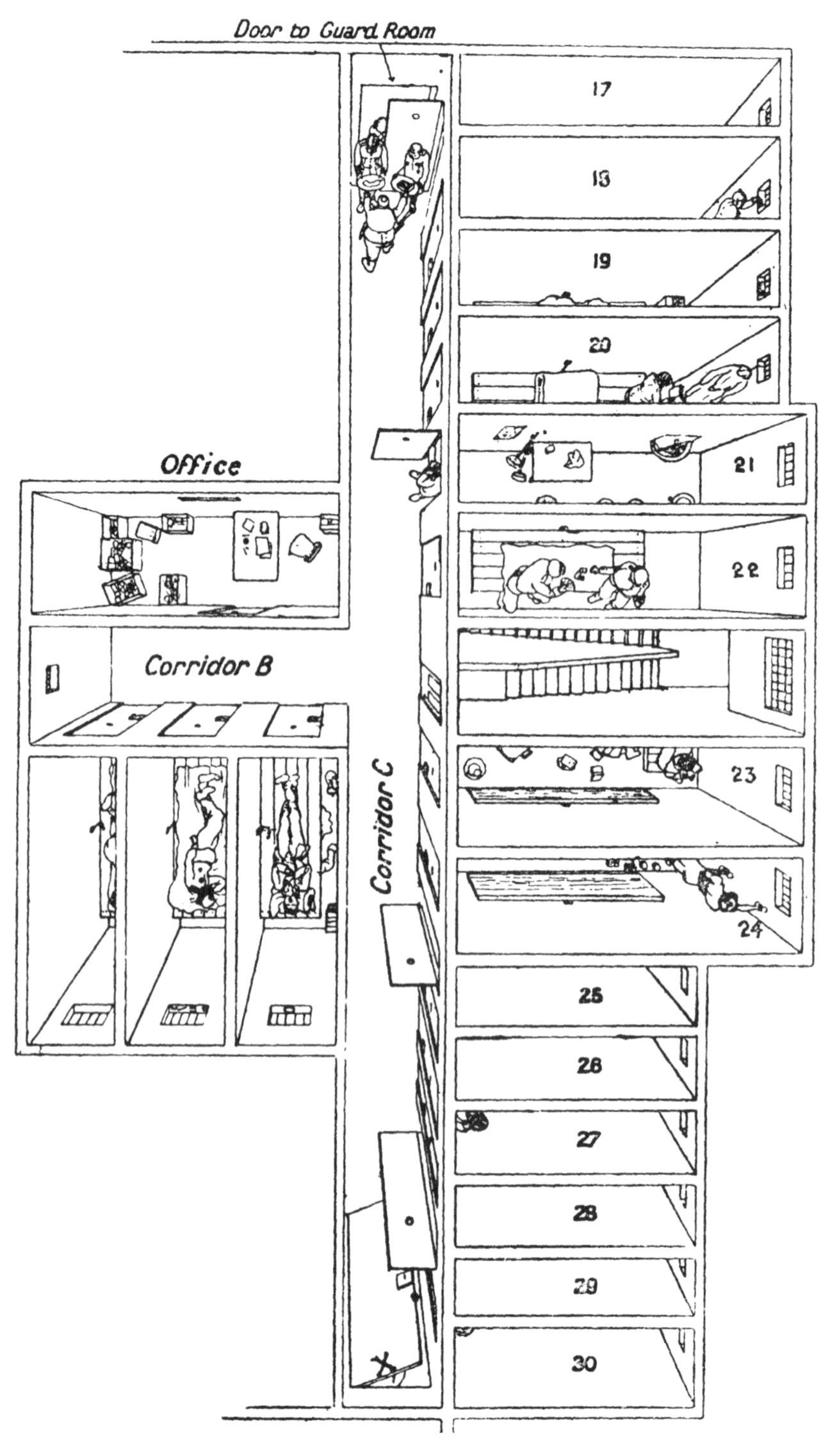

MAGDEBURG PRISON—'KRIEGSGARNISONARRESTANSTALT'

and see that the sentries in the passage never had more than three cell doors open at the same time.

The scheme hinged on this point and required accurate and reliable assistance from two Russian officers and two British, besides temporary inactivity by all the others. Suitable types of sentry and under-officer had to be selected. The guard mounted in the morning, which enabled us to spot beforehand the sentries that would be on duty during the afternoon shifts.

Immediately the orderlies had left the prison, after serving the midday meal, was the time selected. The jailer would be off duty then, so we only had our military guard to contend with.

At 1.45 p.m. on 12th May 1917 every officer was to be in his cell.

At 1.50 the Russian in cell No. 29 was to knock at his door, and as soon as it was opened would tell the sentry he wanted to get a paper from Loder-Symonds in Cell No. 17. The sentry would go with him to open cell No. 17. As they passed cell No. 25 the Russian inside would knock and ask to go to the lavatory (21). The sentry having now opened two cell doors (29 and 25) would be about to open a third (17).

It was impossible for us to open the cell doors from within, so the Russian from cell No. 25 would have our false key in his possession at this moment. He would go as far as the lavatory and leave that door wide open across the corridor. The doors of cells No. 25 and 29, which were slightly smaller than the lavatory door, would also be left open, thus practically blocking the view along the passage from the guard-room.

As No. 29 and the sentry approached cell 17, No. 25 would rush silently back to Cartwright's cell and open it with the false key, which he would leave in the door and return to the lavatory.

Cartwright would come out of his cell (No. 26), lock it with the false key, bolt it, creep along the passage to my cell (No. 28), let me out, re-lock and re-bolt the door. We would then both proceed quietly to the end of the passage, unbolt and unlock, but not open, Campbell's cell (No. 30) and then open and pass through door X.

As we went out we would hand the key to Campbell, who would re-lock door X. Loder-Symonds in cell 17 would do all he could to keep the sentry occupied at the door of his cell as long as possible.

No. 25 could lock and bolt Campbell in his cell and hide the key in the passage before returning to his own cell. Ultimately the sentry would lock and bolt cells 17, 25 and 29, which he himself had opened. All other doors would be already locked and bolted, and, what is more, the key would be back in its original hiding-place.

It can be readily seen that for the success of this scheme silence and rapidity of action were essentials. Our key being rather smaller than the original required most careful manipulation to ensure this. Further, four accomplices had to be well schooled.

The Russian in cell No. 25 had a very important part to play, and making certain, in a language foreign to both him and us, that he thoroughly understood his part was not easy.

Imagine our feelings as we stood in our cells after the midday meal on May 12th fully dressed, waiting for two Russian officers to set the ball rolling. Of course we had blocked our spy-holes, but had the sentry been inquisitive he might at any moment open our doors to remove the obstruction.

Our watches had been carefully synchronised, and on the stroke of time we heard No. 29 knocking. This was a great relief. No. 25 also knocked at precisely the right moment and in another minute had Cartwright's door open. I next heard my own door being stealthily unlocked and I came out to stand close against the wall beside Cartwright. To my horror I noticed the Russian had not left the lavatory door open, so the view down the passage from the guard-room was only partially blocked by the smaller door of cell No. 25.

We now had to exercise the greatest care in getting round the door of cell 29, which was also open.

I went first and unbolted Campbell's door, leaving Cartwright to relock and bolt mine. As soon as he joined me he unlocked Campbell's door, gave me the key and took up a position of observation at the spy-hole of door 29.

He at once reported all was anything but well and that the sentry was walking back toward us.

Nothing but lightning rapidity could save us.

Before I started to tackle door X the sentry must have covered quite half the distance to us. It had evidently been impossible to keep him in conversation at the other end of the passage and he would inevitably have seen us had not Loder-Symonds' last determined effort to entice him back with a bit of food succeeded. As Campbell took the key we walked boldly out. A woman was cleaning the steps on the other side of the door, so, on the spur of the moment, I said '*Malzeit*' over my shoulder, as if speaking to the sentry who had let us out, and we proceeded down the stairs, through the municipal building and out into the street. This time the 'Black Maria' gate was open.

Not knowing how soon we would be missed, we had decided not to leave Magdeburg by any main road. After passing through the town, we followed a track northwards along the bank of the Elbe, longing for a bit of cover into which we could disappear unobserved. Our maps showed a wood about eight kilometres away.

Soon after leaving the town we thought all was lost when a cavalry soldier overtook us, but he rode straight on. Two civilians wearing overcoats on a boiling hot afternoon did not appear to be of interest to him.

We were obliged to keep on our overcoats as our underneath garments were not sufficiently presentable. In addition to his false lapels Cartwright had on an old pyjama coat on to which he had stitched chocolate and other concentrated food. I had a large belt with pockets to take tins in such a position as not to bulge my figure unduly. The remainder of our food, together with my thermos and a 'Tommy's cooker,' we carried in a brown paper parcel. Germans of the class to which we aspired to belong invariably carried brown-paper parcels. Our walk in the heat of the afternoon in this condition was most unpleasant.

At 5 p.m. we were delighted to reach our copse and conceal ourselves. Here we waited till dark re-packing our kit into rucksacks. We had no means of quenching our thirst, and the mosquitoes were almost unbearable.

Before proceeding further it might be as well to narrate the events that occurred in the prison immediately after our departure.

It will be remembered that the adventure started at 1.50, and, interminable as it may have seemed at the time, I don't suppose it was more than three minutes from then before we were through door X.

Campbell shut this door after us, but had not time to lock it.

When the sentry locked the Russian back in cell No. 28 he noticed Campbell's door was unlocked. He just looked in, saw Campbell was inside and locked and bolted it then and there, possibly thinking it might not have been properly shut after the midday meal. At 2 p.m. the sentries were relieved and the new man noticing door X was unlocked opened it, looked out and was seen by the woman, and promptly locked it.

A few minutes later a police sergeant arrived to report that some silly woman had told him that two officers had just escaped. Evidently the charwoman on the stairs had recognized me, as I had passed her several times on my visits to the dentist. The under-officer in charge of the guard was at once woken up, much to his annoyance, and he at once pointed to his row of locked cell doors and told the police sergeant to go away and mind his own business.

Later it was given out that the second sentry was held responsible for our escape and was shot. Whether this was true or whether the man was merely sent elsewhere I cannot say, but it was firmly believed by all subsequent guards.

By 2.5 p.m. all was quiet again and nothing unusual happened till 2.40, when Captain Kunz arrived to inform me that I was to pay three hundred and fifty marks for damage to Government property in Torgau. All efforts to open my cell door failed until a locksmith had been called in, when the door was thrown open to an empty cell. (From previous experience we had discovered that unless the greatest care was used when manipulating our key, the lock was left in such a position that the proper key could not be made to function afterwards.)

When Captain Kunz had recovered from his

first shock he suggested that I must be in Captain Cartwright's cell, and orders were sent to go and see. A further struggle with the lock resulted in the door being flung open ten minutes later to another empty cell.

Captain Kunz' strong point was not an ability to control his temper, and he now gave one of the finest exhibitions imaginable.

He shouted at everybody he could see and ordered all the other cell doors to be opened. He stampeded up and down the passage checking each prisoner himself about half a dozen times in an effort to identify Cartwright and me, and when he had done cursing all the guard he got busy on the telephone. A further invasion by the camp Commandant's staff took place in about ten minutes' time.

The key by now had been restored to its hiding-place in the passage, where it survived all subsequent searches.

Let us now return to our plight in the wood waiting for dark. We had decided to walk to Holland and cross the border in the vicinity of Meppen, where Cartwright and Marshall had been jugged in January.

We had a fair idea how the frontier was guarded and the Emms in this neighbourhood was not a difficult river to swim. An additional point in favour of this area was the probability of being taken to the prison at Meppen in the event of recapture anywhere near the end of our journey.

OFFICERS AND GENTLEMEN

Cartwright knew from experience that this would not be a difficult prison from which to escape. We had both come to the conclusion that no mobilisation was complete unless a reserve compass, map and metal saw could be carried hidden in a place where it would stand a reasonable chance of evading a search in the event of recapture. The map and compass actually in use were almost certain to be confiscated at once, but my thermos flask, which invariably accompanied me, had survived all searches and carried the reserve stores on this occasion. On recapture anywhere in the country a prisoner frequently had a far greater chance of escaping from the local prison than from anywhere else. He was generally only hung up for want of the necessary mobilisation stores.

We had good maps on this occasion, and had planned a definite route of approximately two hundred and twenty-five miles without allowing for walking round villages and towns.

While re-packing in the wood our route card could not be found. Fearing it might have been left in one of our cells, we made out a new one crossing all the rivers by bridges farther north. The new route was just over two hundred and fifty miles. We had only a limited supply of food and the nights were short. Obviously there was no time to be wasted. On both our previous trips we had walked through towns and villages without attracting attention. At this time a night-watchman with fire-arms was kept on duty in every village, but this we did not know at the time of our departure.

We had not intended to pass through any towns or villages west of Cloppenburg, about forty miles from the Dutch frontier, but imagined there would be little danger before reaching that town. In the first village we entered that night a policeman asked us where we were going. Cartwright at once struck a match as if lighting a pipe, kept it lighted quite a time in front of his face showing his collar and tie, and even struck another match, which showed us both to be quite respectable whoever we were. Practically every prisoner who was relying on walking through the country to escape had no alternative but to look like a tramp. Having started with presentable-looking garments we took the greatest trouble to look as tidy as possible. The policeman was quite an interested spectator while Cartwright was struggling with these matches. As we were not prepared to enter into conversation with him, we thought it just as well to show him we were not afraid of being seen. Walking on slowly, we both said '*n'Abend*' which the policeman repeated, evidently satisfied. We noticed in all villages we entered that there was invariably some one about. We could not, on the rations we carried, go round every town and village between us and Holland, but we came to the conclusion that it would be inadvisable to chance any after midnight. If two people were seen walking through a village in the early hours of the morning, and there wasn't another town or village for perhaps eight miles, some suspicion might have been aroused. Even if one was not stopped there was always a possibility of a telephone message being sent to the next place.

This new discovery forced us to start our night journeys rather earlier than we should otherwise have done. Walking through towns and villages just before dusk drew no particular attention to ourselves. Working on Central European time and going due west in May, as we were, meant, however, that every night there was appreciably less darkness before midnight.

Our journey continued for several days without incident. Most days we spent lying amongst small fir-trees, but twice we hid in barns to try and get some rest from the mosquitoes, which were very bad throughout this trip. We were not particularly fit when we left the prison, but our condition improved considerably during the early stages of this journey. We were careful to pay what attention we could to our health, as so many prisoners had previously arrived at the frontier in an exhausted condition and had been recaptured simply through not being physically fit to take due military precautions.

About the fourth night out, while walking round a village, we came in for one of the worst thunderstorms I have ever witnessed. As we lay on our rucksacks in an effort to keep them dry, a house about forty yards away was struck several times and soon burst into flames.

One very dark night my precious hat was lost, but by next day I had made quite a presentable cap out of the seat of my trousers, which was covered by my overcoat.

On the twelfth night out, when we had done about two hundred miles, we were passing through a long, straggly village called Neu Bruchausen. Although it was 10.20 p.m., it was still light and most of the inhabitants were sitting outside their houses. Some of these remembered that two Russian officers had recently escaped from Berxen, a camp about eight miles away on the road by which we had come, and every stranger was a suspect. Soon a crowd of children was following us, and a soldier with obvious intent overtook us, entered into conversation and insisted on our going into the village guard-room, while the entire population collected outside. We were now in the hands of the sorriest-looking collection of congenital idiots ever seen outside a madhouse, and when they took us into a back room and told us to doss down for the night, we had very little doubt that we should be able to give them the slip before morning and go on all the better for the hearty meal, which they were quite prepared to provide—at a price.

As ill-luck would have it, at about midnight a sergeant-major and sergeant of military police dropped in. The military police were of good physique, intelligent-looking and armed to the

SPECIAL CONSTABULARY ABOUT TO BRING OFF A SPECTACULAR ARREST AT NEU BRUCHAUSEN

teeth. These two knew their job and immediately took control. They made a mild search, put us into an old broken-down victoria and told us that we were to be driven to the camp at Berxen. This

THE LANDSTURM WERE NOT VERY BRIGHT BUT——

meant a drive of about eight miles back on the road along which we had come, which, as we knew, passed through a large forest.

It looked as if we should get another chance. I

was put on the box beside the driver, with a coachman's apron fixed over my knees and secured in three places. The two policemen sat on the back seat and Cartwright on the little one in front of

——THE MILITARY POLICE WERE OF GOOD PHYSIQUE, INTELLIGENT-LOOKING AND WELL ARMED

them with his knees wedged between theirs. I had great hopes of being able to jump for it on reaching the forest, thinking the panic would enable Cartwright to follow. From the moment we moved off we were not allowed to speak. Directly I started to move my hand towards the centre fastening of the apron there was a loud roar, the carriage was brought to a standstill and I was secured with a piece of string, the other end of which was held taut by the sergeant-major. Revolvers were cocked, the muzzle of one was pressed against the small of my back and the other against Cartwright's leg, and in this position they remained till we got to Berxen.

On arrival we were brought to the guard-room, which, to our delight, was outside the camp. We still had our reserve maps, compass and metal files, as well as most of the contents of our rucksacks. Imagine our chagrin when we found ourselves locked into a compartment (a cow-stall in better times) in the middle of the guards' building.

Soon after daylight the camp staff had us properly searched. Cartwright managed to save most of his money and the compass we were using, but I lost everything except the thermos, with its valuable contents.

The following day an escort arrived from Magdeburg to bring us back to the civil prison. Practically all our clothes were taken, but both our overcoats were returned after being re-converted into military garments once more. All the military authorities of Magdeburg seemed to be concentrated in the prison during the next fortnight. We were put through an intensive course of questioning from almost every conceivable form of official, and we must have been searched at least three times during this period.

On 6th June Cartwright was transferred to Küstrin.

The following week I was warned for no less than four courts martial on consecutive days. Two were those that I had missed through being out in the country with Cartwright, the others were for appeals against previous trials.

My object now was to amass sufficient punishment to ensure being sent to a 'long-sentence' prison as soon as I gave up appealing. I had great hopes of being sent to Wesel, where officers undergoing long sentences had often been sent in the past. Wesel is close to the Dutch frontier, and Templer had handed me over a plan of the whole fortress with details of a feasible scheme.

At the first court I found my counsel waiting. He had appeared to defend me on the original date selected for this trial, when I had failed to appear. Campbell and Graham-Toler had had to face the charge of damaging the cell at Torgau, and seeing my counsel waiting for me, had asked him to defend them. This he had refused to do, but, strange to relate, they had managed to get an acquittal.

Now, on exactly the same evidence, and with the assistance of a four hundred marks solicitor, I was convicted. The defence in each case was that a fourth occupant, a Russian, had done the damage.

This Russian had been sent to the prison at Burg

the day we came to Magdeburg and there he had found a Belgian (Terlinden, mentioned several times by Cartwright) with everything ready for a train journey to Aachen, and just waiting for a companion. He had written to us from Holland so we knew we could blame him for anything.

I did not employ counsel at any of my other trials.

My account in Germany was now very much overdrawn owing to all the sums that had been deducted for alleged damage to Government property. When I left the country I still had an overdraft, so whether my counsel ever got his four hundred marks or not I do not know. I might here mention that prisoners' accounts were credited with a hundred marks monthly and five pounds was deducted from their army pay.

The other trial I had missed was for 'insulting superior officers by placing an immoral picture in my cell door.' As this was the last time I was tried by court martial in Germany a brief account is perhaps worthy of record. I had prepared a most eloquent defence, referring to well-known pictures of the nude. It was never suggested that these pictures were 'immoral.' Still less should that be the case with the one I had 'hung.' When the artist painted this picture, he took into consideration the possible susceptibilities of those who were likely to see it, and had even gone so far as to allow the model to wear one garment. The prisoner failed to see how anybody but a man with a very vulgar mind could consider it anything but 'artistic.' German thoroughness did not allow any formality to be dispensed with. The picture was passed to the court for each member to study it separately and give his opinion as to whether it was artistic or immoral.

Imagine seven solemn old German officers collected round a bench in full-dress uniform for this purpose at a time when their country was fighting for its very existence.

The court decided it was 'immoral.' Could anything be more unjust? Of course I lodged an appeal, but it never came off. The sentence was five months in prison.

I had now completed eight courts martial, including appeals, and I had no less than seven more on hand, so a word or two about these trials in general might not be amiss.

Each court consisted of from five to seven members and a prosecutor. Appeal courts were similarly constituted. As the same individuals appeared, in different capacities, at most of my trials I believe that one of the reasons for all these courts martial was a desperate effort on the part of these gallant individuals to justify their existence in Magdeburg.

Magdeburg, being about as far as it was possible to get from any front, naturally attracted a large number of self-preservation officers.

A court would seldom allow a trial to be completed without adjourning at least once to decide whether the prisoner was guilty of contempt of court. He invariably was, in their opinion, and before leaving the court the prisoner was usually warned for a further trial.

I used to look forward to my trials with much the same enthusiasm as a theatre-goer might anticipate a new play. After all, it did break the monotony of cell life, and the amount of prison to which I was sentenced did not appear to matter in the least. I seemed doomed to remain in prison indefinitely waiting to start my sentences.

By the time I left Germany I had done thirteen months in prison, not one day of which was to count towards the two years I had amassed. On one occasion when I had to face two trials in the same day there was a short interval after the first when the court had lunch, and I was allowed to leave the room for a few minutes. As my escort led the way, I managed, unobserved, to pick up from the prosecutor's table near the door a large file of documents and conceal them inside my overcoat which I was wearing. I succeeded in depositing these papers in a suitable place before returning to the court. I hoped it meant a lot of extra work for some one. Whether it did or not I cannot say ; I was merely an eye-witness to the annoyance to which the court was put at frequent intervals throughout my trial that afternoon. Every time the file was required a fresh hunt was made for it.

Back in my cell once more after my last trial, I

A COURT MARTIAL

was quite satisfied that I had amassed sufficient imprisonment to justify the authorities sending me to a 'long-sentence' prison directly I gave up appealing, but I could not tear myself away from my beloved key without first satisfying myself that all possibilities had been exhausted.

There were by now only five other officers in this prison; the remainder, having given up appealing, had been sent elsewhere to do their sentences. The guard, however, was not reduced. To guard us six remaining officers in the prison, one officer and twenty-five other ranks were fully employed. Considering we were in one of the most modern prisons in Germany, designed for every type of criminal, we took this as a great compliment.

Great as was our desire to get back to the front and do our bit, we had, at any rate, the satisfaction of knowing that each one of us was occupying on an average over four Germans, apart from our share of the camp Commandant's staff and the court martial officers.

I had my Guards coat, but was otherwise very short of clothes. Fresh supplies of all mobilisation stores were coming rapidly from home. The invisible ink, used principally on special letters which we were ordered to write occasionally instructing those at home not to send certain articles that were forbidden, was doing well. It was also used on cheques and occasional business letters which would be less likely to be thoroughly tested in the censor's office, where all our letters were delayed a fortnight for this purpose. With the help of the ink I arranged a special code which was almost bound to pass, simple as it was. Just every seventh word in an apparently innocent sentence would convey the coded message.

German money was always the greatest necessity, as we were never allowed to have any in our possession. This I was now getting fairly regularly from home, generally sent inside a tube of tooth-paste.

One day when I was parading to watch my parcels being unpacked, I was surprised to see the censor take a tooth-paste tube out of one of my parcels and put it on a shelf behind him. I told him I wanted it immediately, but he informed me that he had been ordered to bring all tooth-paste tubes to the Commandant. Evidently they caught some one else at this game. On returning to my cell I found an unused tube of tooth-paste, which I took back to the office concealed in my hand, and asked the censor if I could make a note of the sort mine was so that I would not be given back the wrong tube. This seemed a reasonable request and it enabled me to exchange tubes. I wrote as soon as I could to stop money being sent this way, but three more tooth-paste tubes must arrive in the meantime. Always appearing with an unused tube of tooth-paste in my pocket I was without difficulty able to arrange an exchange as fresh ones arrived until the last occasion, when Euthymol was sent instead of the customary Kolynos. I now had only a yellow tube to exchange for a white one! I did the exchange, but the censor spotted the trick and rushed after me to my cell. He failed to find the new one, but he did not dare report the incident to the Commandant, knowing that he would get into trouble. Eventually he contented himself by making up his mind that he would not allow it to happen again. No more came.

The examination of parcels was very much stricter than at Torgau. Prisoners were not allowed to receive any tins or rations. The contents required for immediate consumption were put on to a plate and cut up into small pieces by the censor. The remaining tins were kept in the office till required, when the same procedure was followed.

All tins containing contraband in my parcels were specially marked with a secret mark which I alone could recognise, and these I always left in the office. Having the key of the door I could exchange them for other tins when required. As long as the Germans had the right number of tins they were satisfied, so each tin containing contraband also contained a smaller tin to take its place.

And so my mobilisation continued. I had been using invisible ink successfully for over a year, and by now a regular supply of stores was arriving. This enabled me to speed up considerably successive attempts.

By the middle of July I was ready with my new

scheme, but should have to go alone. I was, however, short of trousers, as I had no material which could possibly be made to do. I was reduced to wearing an old pair of breeches and putties.

A most perfect blue mufti suit had arrived from home, covered with red braid, brass buttons, badges of rank, shoulder-straps, etc., etc., but, try as I would, I could not persuade the authorities to let me have it. I completely destroyed the only pair of breeches I had, at first going about in appalling rags and then refusing to take exercise at all because I had not adequate clothes. For how long they would have left me in this state I do not know.

At the end of July we were informed that the British and German Governments had come to an agreement that all prisoners in jail were to be released on 1st August and sent to officers' camps. This was supposed to be great news for us, but it didn't suit me at all. I hated the thought of being separated from my key, and I felt in a very short time I would be able to perfect my present scheme. I pleaded I couldn't possibly go, as I had no clothes, and must wait where I was till fresh ones were sent from home. The Commandant was so overjoyed at the thought of getting rid of me that on the 31st July the blue mufti suit disguised as uniform was given to me. I now felt that during the move on the following day, no matter where they took me, I should have a sporting chance of jumping from the train. My kit was the most perfect imaginable. Still I was not satisfied at the thought of leaving my key without making one more effort with it. It was still out of the question to get away at night, so there only remained the rest of that day. I went down to afternoon exercise all ready, wearing my newly acquired uniform. We were accompanied by an under-officer and sentry as usual.

I have already pointed out that the exercising yard was entirely surrounded by buildings. We entered the yard by a small door at the foot of the stairs in our building. The only other approach was through an archway from the main building; the door in this archway was locked by our jailer immediately before our exercising hour, and on termination he had to unlock it again.

At the foot of the stairs in our building, in addition to the door leading into the yard was a second one leading to a store-room at the back. Our key fitted this door. A previous reconnaissance had revealed the fact that this would be an excellent place in which to do a hasty change, i.e. pull the brass buttons, badges of rank, and red braid off my uniform, and walk out as a civilian across the yard into the street.

On the completion of exercise the sentry led the way upstairs; we six officers followed as slowly as possible and the under-officer brought up the rear. I only had to get through this one locked door before the under-officer got into the building. Although I had opened the door on previous occasions and locked it again, as luck would have it I could not on this occasion do it quickly enough.

I did not let the under-officer catch me at the lock, and I got the key returned to its old hiding-place before we all left the prison on the following day for Ströhen in Hanover. Perhaps I was foolish to make this attempt and risk losing all my beautiful stores and kit, with the prospect of a train journey the following day, which would, at any rate, take me three parts of the way to Holland.

Perhaps I had that feeling at the back of my mind when trying to open the door at the foot of the stairs in a desperate hurry.

So ended a stay of over seven months in one of the smallest cells imaginable, three feet four inches by ten feet six inches.

VI

STRÖHEN

By M. C. C. HARRISON

Description of camp—Plans for escape—The bathroom trapdoor—Preparations for walk to Holland—A nine days' walk—Crossing the frontier—A quarantine camp—ENGLAND.

ON the 1st August 1917, Captain Loder-Symonds, Captain Bowring, Lieut. Campbell and myself were moved from Magdeburg to Ströhen. Before arrival we were not quite certain as to the location of this camp beyond the fact that it was somewhere in the province of Hanover and consequently much nearer Holland. I wanted to attempt to jump off the train on the journey. Wearing my blue suit with detachable red stripes, gold braid, brass buttons and badges of rank, I could not have wished for a more suitable kit. Further, I had a rucksack containing sufficient provisions for a month's walk.

Had the train been going east instead of west, I am sure I would have been out of it before it had gone very far as I had just reached the stage when I was inclined to be desperate. I tried to flatter myself that I was becoming more courageous, but Loder-Symonds opened my eyes by warning me that it was just the courage of despair, and implored me not to do anything rash. I accordingly pulled myself together for the train journey, and although opportunities of a sort did occur I sat where I was and let the train take me nearer Holland, hoping for a better opportunity later on.

We were agreeably surprised to find our destination was nearer Holland than we had expected, and shortly before the end of our journey I all but made a jump for it. The only risk appeared to be that I might damage myself in the fall and be unable to walk. I summed it up as an even money chance and worth the risk, but I allowed myself to be overruled by the advice of the majority. They argued that we were being taken to a camp comparatively near the frontier where better opportunities might exist.

The camp of Ströhen, about eighty miles as the crow flies from Holland, was situated in a swamp extending for miles in all directions. It consisted of a series of dilapidated wooden huts, surrounded by inner and outer high barbed-wire fences five yards apart, each of the four sides being about two hundred yards long, and it had been built originally as a reprisal camp for Russian officers. This was to be our home for an indefinite period, and the mere sight of it on arrival would have had a most depressing effect on us had not our thoughts been otherwise engaged. Almost from the moment it came into view our minds began to work on the old problem: 'How the devil are we going to get out of the place?' Personally I did not like the idea of being surrounded by barbed-wire fences only, for this enabled sentries on both sides to see what the prisoners were doing.

The Commandant was one of the most unpleasant individuals that I have ever come across. Mercifully his brutality was equalled by his inefficiency. So drastic was his treatment of prisoners who defied his authority in any way that I believe he was considered a most suitable Commandant for a reprisal camp.

When we arrived, there were about four hundred and fifty English and a few native Indian officers in the camp, but no one of any other nationality, thus minimising the danger of spies. Up to now I had only been in camps occupied mostly by our Allies and I had not met more than thirty-six English officers altogether since my capture. Amongst the four hundred and fifty in Ströhen I discovered several pre-war friends, and quite a number of hardened criminals in the eyes of the Germans.

In spite of the brutalities perpetrated by the Commandant, the spirit of the prisoners and loyalty to our Sovereign were better than I have ever seen.

Although the Germans from without could see into the camp through the barbed-wire fences, they strongly resented any of the prisoners stopping to look at them. This frequently resulted in the camp Commandant ordering the guard into the camp to charge the prisoners with fixed bayonets.

During the week after my arrival two such raids took place and two British officers were wounded and removed to hospital. I myself only escaped on one of these occasions by parrying with an arm a determined bayonet thrust, the point going through my coat and sticking in the wooden hut against which I was standing. The sentry experienced so much difficulty in extracting it that I managed to tear myself away before he was able to have another thrust at me.

The raid was brought to an end in a sensational manner. A prisoner with a gramophone put on a 'National Anthem' record, whereupon every prisoner stood to attention and sang each verse of 'God Save the King' as loud as he could. The tune being the same as that of a popular German patriotic song, and the guard, not realising what was happening, stood still as well. The Commandant, fuming and shouting orders from without, failed to make himself heard owing to the noise the prisoners were making.

Finding so many old friends and such a fine collection of gallant officers, my first consideration was to select a companion for my next attempt. Templer was in this camp and had already arranged to go with two other officers, both unknown to me. They had more or less completed a plan to get out via the parcel room enclosure, which corner of the camp was not particularly strongly guarded, as it was wired off from the rest and was out of bounds to all prisoners except during one hour in the morning. They consented to bring me with them, but as there were several hitches to be overcome we decided to see if we could think of a better plan.

Although the dimensions of the camp are immaterial I am making a rough sketch drawn from memory to illustrate the general lay-out and essential features from the prisoner's point of view.

As the camp was originally intended for reprisal purposes, the space for exercise and recreation was made as small as possible by keeping the inner barbed wire fence close to the huts where the prisoners lived. Such buildings as the guard-room and even the bathroom hut were outside the camp fortifications. Access for prisoners to the latter building was allowed between 8.30 and 9.30 every morning, when a portion of the guard was on special duty there.

One part of the bathroom hut was intended for the use of Germans only and the entrance for this portion faced the guard-room (see plan). The other part was divided into three rooms, i.e. one for heating appliances, one containing six or eight showers, and the third measuring about twelve feet by ten feet was used as a dressing-room. The entrance to this portion faced the camp and was connected to a gate in the inner fence by a wired-in passage.

It was obvious to every one that if a prisoner could remain concealed in the bathroom building

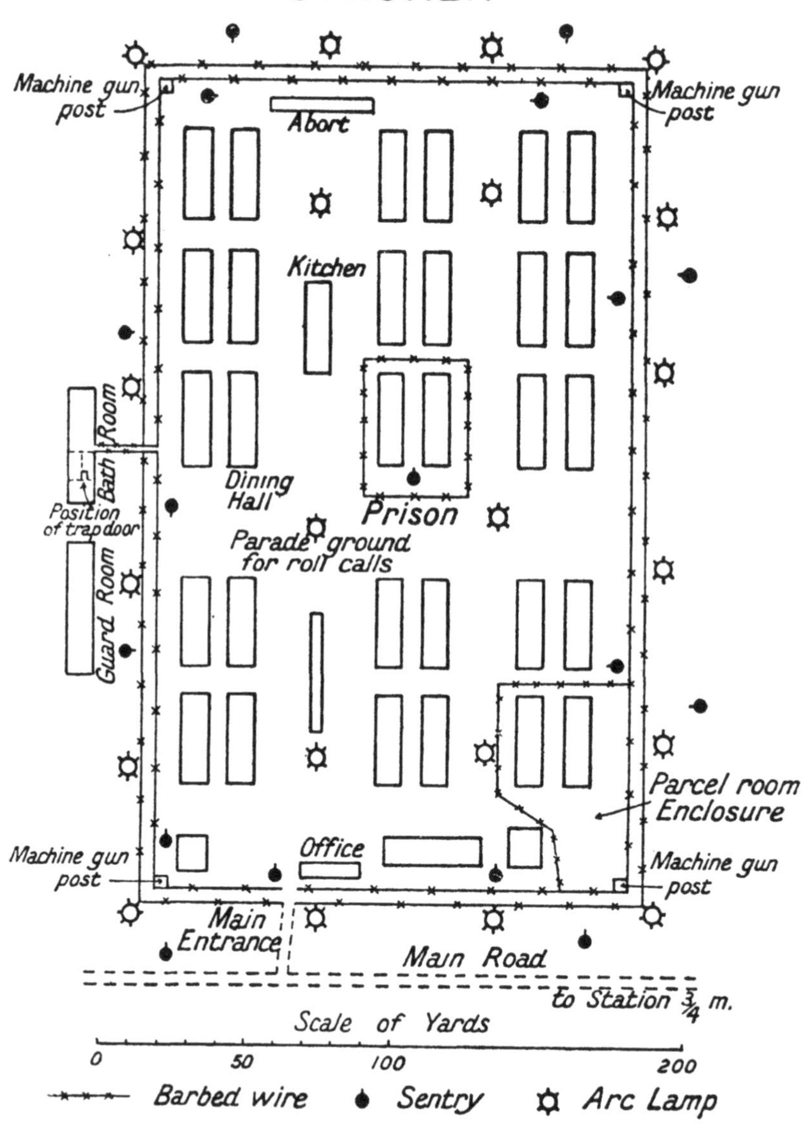
STRÖHEN
Machine gun post
Machine gun post
Abort
Kitchen
Bath Room
Position of trap door
Guard Room
Dining Hall
Prison
Parade ground for roll calls
Parcel room Enclosure
Machine gun post
Office
Machine gun post
Main Entrance
Main Road
to Station ¾ m.
Scale of Yards
0
50
100
200
Barbed wire
Sentry
Arc Lamp

until dark he would have practically no further difficulty, as he would be outside the camp fortifications and line of sentries. The Germans guarded against this eventuality by keeping sentries in all three rooms to which the prisoners had access during the hour available for baths.

As a precaution against tunnelling they took special steps to see that no revetting material was available, and they also examined the floors of all buildings daily.

There was nothing to be gained by being sent to prison, as the cells were in a special hut, surrounded by wire, in the centre of the camp.

Unlike either of my previous camps, Ströhen contained a large number of officers who were looking out for a feasible means of escape. Most of them had already done time for previous attempts, and were engaged working out fresh plans. It was an unwritten law that if anyone got to hear of some one else's plan they would not only abstain from interfering but would render any assistance required. Watched as we were it was out of the question to appoint a special control board for organising all escapes.

At the end of the week we decided to concentrate on the bathroom.

The floor was raised about six or eight inches from the ground, so that if we scooped away sufficient earth from under part of it we would be able to conceal ourselves.

By feeling with wire between the planks we found a corner of the dressing-room was clear of all supports and would be a suitable place for a trap-door.

The plan was simple and straightforward, the only disadvantages being that directly we started work the whole camp would know all about it, and we could only work for a very short time each day.

Between 8.45 and 9.15 a.m. the dressing-room was always crammed, and this would help to block the sentries' view and stop them hearing the noise of our saw. Only one of our party could work at a time; the remaining three would either dry themselves with large towels in front of the nearest sentry or make a noise with their boots on the floor.

The only other precaution to be taken was to disguise the fact that planks were being cut as the authorities examined the bathroom floor daily as well as all floors inside the camp.

By experimenting, in another building, we discovered that the desired effect could be attained by rubbing into the cut a solution of seccotine and dust and this is how we proposed to cover our tracks each day.

It took us four days to saw through two planks, which was sufficient for our trap-door. On the fifth and sixth days we scooped away the earth in the vicinity of the trap-door with an arm. All this was most precarious, as we were working from above. On the seventh day we had sufficient earth removed to enable one man to get inside and carry on work with the trap-door shut on top of him. From now on as soon as the dressing-room was full we sent one of our number, absolutely naked, through the trap-door, and let him up in sufficient time to wash himself and get out of the bathroom before closing time.

By the 14th August our work was nearing completion; we had almost scooped away sufficient earth to accommodate three people when one of our party asked to be excused from continuing. He was a young officer of the best type imaginable; but a senior officer, also a very good fellow, had advised him not to take the risk. We had just had another instance of the camp Commandant's brutality, and this senior officer was of opinion that if we were found lying under the bathroom floor the guard would certainly bayonet us. As we had to remain concealed there for so long, he didn't think we had a chance of evading detection during the exhaustive search that would take place directly we were missed. We would be present at the 8.30 morning roll-call, but as there were four of us we could not hope to bluff the one at 6 p.m. Templer had already made a large number of attempts at escape and was believed to be somewhat reckless. I had, in a minor degree, possibly acquired the same reputation, whereas Insall, a Flying Corps V.C. subaltern, might easily prove to be still more daring.

As we formed three of the party, no one can blame

the fourth for acting on the advice he received from a really fine senior British officer, who had made more than one attempt himself and who believed the present scheme to be unsound. That there is on question of this officer 'funking it' at the last moment is evident from the fact that he volunteered to do everything in his power to help us—even to cut the wire on the other side of the camp to make the Germans think we had gone that way.

We considered it would be a wise precaution to give the Germans a false clue as to how we had gone since they were bound to miss us. On our absence being discovered we knew a search would take place to see if they could find out how we had gone, and we feared that our trap-door, though sufficiently concealed for the casual routine searches, might not be adequately camouflaged to be proof against a specially organised one.

We were very sorry to lose our friend, and I am quite certain he would have continued if by so doing it would have helped us in any way.

A serious hitch occurred the same day. We discovered that another pair had attempted to make a trap-door elsewhere in the dressing-room. We at once interviewed them and found out that they had come upon bricks underneath and proposed making another trap-door. Our party was very disgusted, and we felt that they would ruin our chances. We were of opinion that they had copied our idea and were trying to beat us on time; they on the other hand were firm that they had worked entirely on their own initiative and meant to see their plan through. As it was out of the question to have the whole floor covered with trap-doors, we compromised by agreeing to make room for the two additional people in our compartment. This delayed our departure by three or four days.

On the 17th August we had another shock. Lieut. Knight, Devons and R.A.F., had on the 16th effected a successful escape via the bathroom, and, if the Germans discovered how he had gone, there wasn't a hope for us. Fortunately he had concealed his tracks well. Going in with the crowd on the 16th he stood in a recess in one wall about ten inches deep and one foot wide. He brought in under his coat three long canvas frames whitewashed the colour of the wall, which were just wide enough to cover the recess and fitted into each other. He built these up in front of himself unobserved and stood behind the camouflage for twelve hours. Although several Germans went into the bathroom during the day he remained concealed.

By the 19th August 1917 we had made sufficient space for five people and decided to go the next day.

Lieut. Onslow, Warwickshire Regiment, volunteered to seal our trap-door after we had got into position, and he proposed to bring a party through the same way later on.

On the 20th we arrived in the bathroom, fully mobilised, getting a certain amount of assistance to help us to carry in all our stores unobserved. I was the first to be let through the trap-door and was given the job of storing all the kit in prearranged compartments on the side farthest from the guard-room. We were somewhat concerned about the ventilation, as a small hole at the guard-room end seemed to be the only means of getting any fresh air. By 9 a.m. we were all in position with the trap-door securely sealed on top of us. Throughout the day we could hear the Germans coming into the bathroom, mostly just to look for soap, which was, by now, almost unobtainable in Germany. We could easily distinguish the inspecting party examining the floor. Realising the tediousness of this long wait, we provided ourselves with plenty of light refreshments, but, as expected, the air soon became stifling. I was close to the air hole so had nothing to complain of in this direction compared to Insall, who was farthest away from it.

At 6 p.m. the bugle sounded for the evening roll-call and we were now going to be missed.

On my previous attempts it had always been a great regret that I could not also witness the scene that took place when my absence was first discovered. Now I was going to get the full benefit of it, as the entrance to the guard-room was less than ten yards from where I lay. The roll-call, as might be expected, took longer than usual, but soon the sound of guttural explosions could be heard coming from the camp. This was followed by great activity in the guard-room. From where

I lay I could even get a glimpse of them all being turned out on to the parade-ground not five yards from me. The Commandant himself came down and, stampeding up and down in front of them, shouted out his orders. Detachments were sent off to search various parts of the camp and the bathroom.

We heard sentries again overhead, but just as they entered the building another roar was let forth by the Commandant, who by now had worked himself up into a real frenzy at the entrance to the guard-room. This time he was shouting for all the guard except sentries on normal duty to return to the guard-room at once.

Evidently they had found a clue, and we presumed it was the cut wire. Patrols were sent off in all directions and a proper hunt was organised for us in the country.

We were certainly getting good value for our money this time.

About 10.30 p.m. we heard shots fired not very far away; probably one of the patrols had lost its way and run into another.

Military activity continued till well after midnight, but as all seemed quiet at 2 a.m. we started to emerge from our hiding-place back into the bathroom through the trap-door.

Once there we completely dressed ourselves for our journey with the exception that we carried our boots so as to be certain of making no noise.

It was a great relief to get fresh air again after lying in a cramped position for over seventeen hours on the damp ground underneath the floor.

With the light from the arc lamps we easily located the nearest sentries and watched their movements.

As the expert lock-picker I was given the job of opening the door on the side farthest from the camp. I did not expect the least difficulty, as the lock was of the simplest type and to open it from the inside was child's play. It had always been locked when we were having baths, and as I did not believe the door was ever used I was surprised to find it unlocked now. Opening the door quietly, I could neither see nor hear any sign of danger on this side. Remaining in observation I sent an 'all clear' message back to those who were watching the other side. Directly the sentries had got to a favourable position we crept through my door, still carrying our boots, and walked away from the camp keeping the bathroom between us and the nearest sentry. When about fifty yards from the camp we put on our boots and divided into our respective parties, Insall and Templer coming with me and the other two going on their own.

Beyond the fact that this latter pair were recaptured I know nothing of their adventures.

It was 3 a.m. before we were properly under way and it was going to be daylight in another two hours. We knew there were patrols out looking for us, so our first consideration was to find somewhere to conceal ourselves. The country was boggy and we expected movement might at any time be confined to tracks, so therefore did not walk in the obvious direction towards Holland, but elected to go north till we were clear of the swamp. The going was very heavy, and well before daylight we hid ourselves as best we could in a small plantation only a few miles from the camp.

I will now give a brief description of the preparations we made for our walk to Holland.

We had all made previous attempts with other people so could take lessons from practical experience gained on many different occasions.

The following are the main points on which we agreed :

1. We must arrive near the frontier physically fit to take all military precautions.
2. We must make a certainty of finding a good hiding-place every day.
3. If we disagreed over any point when we were out, we would abide by the majority, and in the event of all three disagreeing, we would adopt the course which was least likely to lead to immediate recapture. Most people escaping in pairs had experienced difficulty in settling some point, where to hesitate was obviously the worst thing to do.
4. We decided to avoid main roads, towns and villages, and to swim rivers unless a careful

reconnaissance revealed the fact that a bridge was unguarded. In fact, to avoid letting anyone see us throughout our journey.

I had a certain amount of difficulty in establishing the last point, as both Insall and Templer spoke the language exceptionally well and were confident that they would only have to talk to each other in German to avert suspicion.

To take all these precautions would obviously be a slow job, but we were determined to profit by all our practical experience and take no unnecessary risk.

Our kit on this occasion was consequently of comparatively little importance, but it is interesting to note that for the third time I escaped in my much disguised Guards officer's overcoat.

Instead of encumbering ourselves with a quantity of tinned food we carried a Tommy's cooker, a small saucepan and a large supply of solid methylated spirits. The only actual food we started with was chocolate for use at night, biltong (dried meat used largely in South Africa), bacon, porridge and a few biscuits. A football bladder did duty as a water bottle and of course I brought my thermos flask containing spare maps, compass and metal files.

We had all discovered that it was quite easy to carry sufficient nourishment for a long journey, but that lack of bulk at all meals was very trying and frequently resulted in proper safety precautions not being taken. We now decided to loot fresh vegetables at night, which would enable us to have an excellent hot stew every day, and keep to a more or less normal diet. It would retard our marches at night, but this was more than outweighed by the advantage of approaching the frontier in a really fit condition.

As we had arranged to get off our bog on the north side, we decided to make for Holland as far north as possible before the Emms became too wide to swim. This would make our march about one hundred and twenty miles.

The Emms flows more or less parallel to the frontier in this area, and is about six or seven miles inside Germany. The intervening country is marshy, and we had gathered a certain amount of information as to the manner in which the frontier was guarded. Recaptured prisoners told us that in addition to a line of sentries on the frontier itself all bridges over the river were watched, and that the intervening country was believed to be unguarded. The Emms was only about fifty yards wide, and from its twisty course on the map it was obvious the current was slow and that it should be easy to swim.

Another advantage in this area was the fact that the frontier was practically a straight line running north and south, so there should be no danger of walking into Germany again after crossing it, as had been done by some one else in the camp.

The boundary was not clearly defined on the ground, but just inside this part of Holland and parallel to the frontier for several miles, a dyke was shown on our map, and this would give us a clearly-defined objective on the ground to make for.

Let us now turn to our plight in the country. Our first day in the plantation passed slowly as we had no occupation, not even cooking, to help to pass the time and we were still unpleasantly close to the camp. We did not anticipate any great danger in being discovered by the dogs that were out looking for us, as we had taken the precaution to cover our feet and ankles with garlic, which no dog will follow.

As expected, the mosquitoes were really bad, but my precautions against them were adequate. Remembering the awful time they had given me on previous occasions I now carried my provisions in a sack instead of the customary rucksack, and I slept inside this during the day. Templer and Insall were not quite so fortunate, and took turns to sleep in my sack, sometimes both sleeping in it at the same time.

At 10.30 p.m. we moved off, again going in a northerly direction, and found good cover, still on the marsh, for the next day.

The third night we got badly bogged before we eventually got clear of the swamp.

Throughout the fourth night a fierce thunderstorm raged and the rain continued well into the next day.

Up to now we had made extremely slow progress and on the fifth night, marching due west, in spite of our good resolutions we nearly made the fatal mistake of not seeking cover soon enough. Shortly before 5 a.m., at which hour it would be light, we were greatly relieved to find a small copse which appeared to be a good hiding-place. After daylight we discovered we were lying dangerously close to a woodman's cottage. There was now no alternative but to get as far away from this building as we could without exposing ourselves, but we could not get farther than twenty-five yards from it. So imminent was the danger that we did not dare unpack anything or even take off our boots. Soon the occupants were up and about, and, to our horror, a dog amongst them. We at once got busy with the garlic, which we continued to rub all day. How we kept the animal at bay I cannot understand, but shortly after 9 p.m., quite an hour before dark, he smelt us and gave tongue. Before anyone could take action we moved away from all habitation, knowing that darkness would soon come to our assistance. That night and the next there were many small rivers and streams to cross, but in every case we were either able to wade through them or find unguarded bridges without going near main roads.

On the seventh night we got so hopelessly bogged that we had to retrace our steps for several miles and select another route very much farther south; and before daylight we found what I should imagine to be the best cover I have ever been in. It was a large wood consisting of pine-trees of various heights.

Selecting a batch about six feet high near the middle, we were more than satisfied with our find, for up to now we had never come across such ideal cover.

About 11 a.m. a woodman arrived to prune those very trees in which we lay. We kept perfectly still, hoping he would not come sufficiently close to see us, but after about twenty minutes he spotted us and ran away to get assistance.

Had we detained this man the probability is others would have come to look for him later on, so we decided to pretend we were tramps having a rest. We took special care to show no sign of surprise when he noticed us ; in fact, our intention was to let him think we had not seen him and at any rate were not going to move. We could hear him running away, and as soon as his footsteps had died in the distance we were up and away in the opposite direction, covering ourselves with garlic and throwing pepper on all surrounding ground. We guessed the whole wood would be searched, so before the alarm could be spread we walked across country to another forest about one and a half miles away.

As most people about, at that hour in the morning, had some definite object in view, the probability was that our walk across the intervening fields would cause no undue suspicion if accomplished before the alarm was spread.

Once in our new wood we were completely covered from view to any search-party that might by now be looking for us. Sooner or later this party would in all probability get information that we had been seen entering the forest we were now in, so we made for the farthest end, choosing a very thick clump of trees in a slight depression in which to hide. With a pocket-knife we dug sods and heather out of the earth and placed them on top of us as we lay there, giving the impression of a slight rise in the ground instead of a hollow.

No search-party could find us now unless some one actually put a foot on top of us, and we were quite confident that dogs would not be able to follow us owing to the garlic.

From now on we always adopted the following routine: With one halt for light refreshments and to collect vegetables for the next day, we walked as fast as we could from 11 p.m. to 3 a.m., and then stopped in the first good cover we could find. On arrival we slept at once from sheer exhaustion till the cold woke us up just before dawn. As soon as it was daylight we moved to the best place in our cover, boiled water for breakfast and dug large sods which we left beside us in case of emergency, when we could lie down and place them over us. This exercise got us nice and warm for breakfast, which consisted of porridge, tea, bacon and fried potatoes. This meal took some time as we had only one Tommy's cooker for the three of us. Directly it was over we started to prepare our lunch by peeling potatoes and cutting up the biltong. The other vegetables that went into our stew consisted of cabbage, beet-root, mushrooms or anything else we found the previous night. We never stinted ourselves over this meal, which was generally finished about midday.

We would sleep in the heat of the afternoon till the cold of evening woke us up. Then we would have some tea from a thermos and prepare a light supper on the same lines as the midday meal, always moving off with a hot drink in the thermos for the middle of the night.

Living on this diet, it is not surprising that our physical condition improved daily in spite of the bad weather.

Quite the best find was when we discovered outside a small farm a can of milk presumably left for a dairyman to collect in the morning. It was unfortunate we had just had a drink of water, but nevertheless we all drank as much as we possibly could and filled our football bladder and thermos flask.

Many of my readers may find it difficult to realise how much we appreciated that milk. To get the true effect it would be necessary to go without fresh milk for three years. Think of the improvement to our porridge the next morning. So much did we enjoy it that we resolved to keep our eyes open for a similar find later on.

Failing to find any more milk in cans, we decided to try our luck milking a cow, but unfortunately the first animal we accosted turned out to be a bull and very much resented the liberty we were taking.

When he was fully awake he made it quite clear that he wasn't going to tolerate our presence any longer, and we only escaped from his field with many torn clothes.

The only other time in my life when I tried to milk a cow was in a barn during my first escape with Cartwright in 1915, when I failed for the same reason. As these operations were carried out in darkness I consider it was sheer bad luck.

It poured with rain throughout the eighth night, when we were once more in boggy country and had many serious obstacles to negotiate in the way of flooded drains. We were rewarded by finding excellent cover at the end of it, about one mile south-east of Melstrup. Wet as we were it certainly was a great relief to get a day's rest free from worry. Up to the present we had experienced really bad weather, and the flooded nature of the marshy ground had added considerably to our fatigue.

We were now only about six miles from the Emms, and had we been in poor condition or really hungry we would probably have tried to cross the frontier the following night. Sticking to our resolution to take no unnecessary risks we spent the ninth night reconnoitring the approaches to the river and selecting a suitable place to swim it.

One or two tributaries and small streams made the approach march slow, and it was 2 a.m. before we reached the river in the vicinity of Fresenburg. Here it was about forty-five yards wide, with cover on both sides suitable for undressing and dressing.

Knowing Holland was only six miles away and believing the intervening country was unwatched it was very tempting to swim across at once and rush for the frontier.

We adhered to our good resolution and retraced our steps to the last suitable cover we had found.

The ninth day we spent studying our maps until we knew by heart all the features between us and the frontier, and we remained in hiding till 11 p.m.

We reached the river at 11.45 p.m. Templer and Insall wrapped their clothes tightly inside a waterproof, which they cut up, and put the bundles into their rucksacks, I put my clothes and boots into my sack. We all kept our hats on our heads, with watches and compasses inside. Before entering the water we listened to make certain that no patrols were approaching.

I was surprised at the rapidity with which Templer and Insall got across, the rucksacks strapped to their backs merely floating on the surface and acting as a support. My sack, on the other hand, got soaking wet and really heavy, but I managed to drag it across slowly.

Soon after midnight we were dressed again on the western side. It was not going to be light till 5 a.m., and we had only six miles to go ; we didn't expect any opposition till we reached the frontier, but as we had plenty of time at our disposal we took all possible precautions.

Before swimming the river we had discarded our stores and surplus kit, and we now abandoned our sack and rucksacks so as to carry no unnecessary weight.

The precautions we now took appeared superfluous in view of the information we had collected in Ströhen that the country would not be guarded till the actual frontier was reached.

One of us advanced in front of the other two and lay down every thirty yards to scan the horizon. As this was the tenth consecutive night that we had been out, our vision was probably better than that of sentries, who were never on duty for more than two consecutive hours. We advanced in this formation for about two miles when to our surprise we saw a sentry. We decided to go ahead, keeping as close to this man as we could so as to minimise the chances of running into an unseen neighbouring one.

When we were manœuvring round this man, the moon came out suddenly from behind a cloud and compelled us to lie down flat where we were, beside a cabbage patch. The sky previously overcast, now became clear and bright but knowing the moon would set at about 2.30 a.m. we decided to remain where we were lying flat, with our faces and hands covered, till then. It was a little before 1 a.m. at the time, and as we lay there for nearly two hours, two lots of relief sentries or patrols walked along a track within five yards of where we lay, with nothing whatever between us and them ; even the cabbages were on the other side of us.

At 2.45 a.m. we continued the movement we had

attempted two hours previously. There were several wire fences to climb, and when we were negotiating one of these about two or three hundred yards beyond the sentry we had located, we rang an alarm bell in a neighbouring building.

As the first of us rang the bell in climbing the fence the other two rushed forward and got over, and we all lay down to watch. Almost immediately we saw a sentry leave the building where the bell had rung and proceed along a road running north and south about ten yards in front of us, presumably to rouse the rest of the guard. As soon as he had passed we crossed this road and continued as rapidly as we could. We disturbed some young horses in the next field, but this evidently conveyed nothing to the sentry, who was concerned in nothing but carrying out his orders to the letter. When we were about thirty yards beyond the road we lay down again to see what was happening and noticed electric lamps moving along the wire fence we had just climbed. Whatever the opposition was here, we had evidently got through it, but having caused an alarm we now proceeded to get away from it as quietly as we could.

During the next few hundred yards we had to negotiate eight or ten ditches waist deep in water with wire on top. This could only be done quietly by going right under water and coming up the other side of the wire. These ditches I should imagine were purely intended for drainage purposes, and having negotiated the last about 3 a.m. we had now two hours of darkness in which to cover nearly four miles.

The situation which a short time ago had looked very black now appeared most favourable.

The country was marshy, obviously too heavy to be patrolled in the ordinary course of events, but not enough to impede us seriously ; the stars were shining so there was no chance of losing direction, and there was a slight head wind which minimised the chances of the sentries on the frontier hearing us as we approached.

We continued the march as before with one in front lying down every thirty yards. Our vision was by now excellent and we were in high spirits.

After about three miles we came across some more drainage ditches. We saw two sentry huts about sixty yards apart and steered midway between them. Once we crossed a perfectly dry ditch which we thought might be the frontier. We must have gone through about ten or twelve deep ditches before we came to firm land again and each time we crossed a large ditch with any sort of a bank we thought perhaps that it was the dyke, shown on our map just inside Holland.

It is a well-known fact that you do not cover the ground on these occasions as quickly as you imagine, and prisoners have been known to give themselves up when they were still in Germany thinking they were well over the frontier. The Dutch guards were also believed to be capable of handing escaping prisoners back to the Germans for a small reward, so we resolved to avoid the Dutch as well as the German frontier guards and go on walking due west till daylight.

For quite half a mile we must have enjoyed the glorious uncertainty of not knowing whether we really had crossed the frontier or not.

At 4.30 a.m. the 4th September 1917, while in this state of uncertainty, I saw what appeared to be a cloud in the west with a perfectly horizontal border. At first there was nothing particularly strange in this sight as it was so dim, but I soon could discern a perfectly cut V in it. For a moment I wondered if the strain had begun to tell on my nerves, then I realised it was a bank about thirty foot high with a gap in it.

'The dyke in Holland beyond a shadow of doubt.'

As the reality dawned on me I formed my idea of 'the finest view in Europe.'

The gap was about eighty yards away in front of me and, expecting to find the Dutch guard in that vicinity, we climbed the bank about two hundred yards farther south and swam the canal on the western side of it.

Although we knew for certain we were now in Holland we walked with a light foot for two more hours, getting as far from Germany as we could before demanding breakfast at some inn. During those two hours we could hardly imagine there was such a thing as fatigue.

Breakfast at Terhaar was a great meal; the inn-keeper and his wife were both charming, but in accordance with Dutch regulations on the crossing of the frontier in an irregular manner, they were obliged to hand us over to the military for removal to a quarantine camp at Enschede.

The trains were not good and our escort arranged to spend the night at Coevorden. Here, in spite of our protests, we were handed over to the local police and were locked up in a large cell containing a bucket, a little straw, a lot of bugs, and two German deserters. Protests during the next few hours merely led to assurances that all would be well at our quarantine camp.

After four hours' agitation a junior Dutch officer arrived on the scene and he, realising we did not mean to be trifled with, gave us permission to spend the night in the hotel, on condition that we gave our parole not to escape and would be ready to move off at 5.30 a.m. the following morning.

We readily agreed and were escorted down the town in our wet rags of clothes followed by a huge crowd of white-haired children. A mixture of German and English got us most of the garments we required at a small stores, but it was not till we were changing for dinner that we discovered that, instead of buying shirts with collars attached, we had come away with ladies blouses. They barely reached as far as the top of our trousers and the sleeves were decidedly short, but we managed to dress ourselves to our satisfaction. At the champagne dinner which followed we noticed the four daughters of the manager were dressed in similar garments.

I do not know what hour it was when we went to bed, but I have seldom felt so comfortable in my life, and I seemed to have hardly got there when I had to get up again.

It is apparently a fault common to all nations to get troops out of bed in the middle of the night whenever a move is necessary.

The quarantine camp at Enschede was full of German deserters. Knight, who had escaped from Ströhen, via the bathroom, four days before us was also there, and he was delighted to see us.

In spite of many protests we were kept here eleven days before being moved to Rotterdam and thence to ENGLAND.

I leave it to my readers to imagine the welcome that awaited us from our friends at home. During our first week in London we had the honour of being summoned to Buckingham Palace, where His Majesty was pleased to listen to our experiences. On the day that I went His Majesty was occupied with an Investiture that lasted the whole morning, and immediately afterwards he honoured me with a half-hour's private interview in a small room.

Could any loyal subject wish for a greater honour ?

VII

KÜSTRIN, SCHWEIDNITZ AND AACHEN

By H. A. CARTWRIGHT

Fort Zorndorf—The communication tunnels—Courts martial in Berlin—Tricks that failed—German military justice—A successful appeal—A good Prussian—The Russians at Zorndorf—Move to Schweidnitz—Plans for escape—Transfer to Aachen—Escaping from Aachen—An out-of-date map—The frontier at last—Rotterdam—The War Office—The Armistice.

IN Chapter V Harrison has told the story of our life in Magdeburg police prison and the attempts which we made to escape from it, and I now have to take the story on from the point where I was moved from the prison.

On 6th June 1917 I was moved (thanks to the intervention of the Dutch Minister) to Fort Zorndorf, Küstrin. On arrival there I learnt from the English prisoners that Harrison was to follow me the next day—the Germans wouldn't let us travel together—but, as it happened, I filled the last bed in the camp and he was therefore sent to Ströhen, whence he reached England in something like record time.

Küstrin is a fortress in Brandenburg, some hundreds of kilometres east of Berlin. It is more than five hundred kilometres from the Dutch and six hundred from the Swiss frontier. Fort Zorndorf is an underground fort, one of a ring built in the 'eighties and paid for by part of the French war indemnity, and was just about as impossible to get out of as a prison camp can be. It is bounded on all sides by a forty foot dry ditch, having a perpendicular brick wall on the outside, and over two hundred soldiers were employed to guard a hundred prisoners. This fact alone should, I think, justify the escape maniac as against the scoffer. It is true that those two hundred soldiers were a pretty sorry lot, but every one of them could have been doing a more useful job and so have released a better man for a job nearer the front. If the Germans had guarded all their prisoners with the same strictness that they guarded the few bad characters at Küstrin and similar strong camps, quite an appreciable reduction would have been made in their fighting strength.

I found at Küstrin about twenty Englishmen who had attempted to escape from other camps and some eighty Russians, nearly all of the baser sort. When Russians are base they are very base, and these were mostly thieves, murderers, habitual drunkards or otherwise unpleasant. This may look like exaggeration, but it is literally true. While I was at Magdeburg a Russian murdered a brother-officer in cold blood. He was tried and sentenced to two months' imprisonment and returned to the same camp after serving his time. He was quite well received by the rest of the Russians and was a great success among the French, who used to arrange tea-parties 'to meet M. l'assassin.' He was not the only murderer in the camp.

The French had achieved the removal of their officers from the fort, which was unfit for prolonged human habitation, by practising reprisals on the prisoners in their hands.

There was a rule that no prisoner was to be kept at Zorndorf for more than four months unless he incurred the displeasure of the local military authorities, when he might have his term extended by another quarter. Most of the English finished their time soon after my arrival and only a few others came to take their places, the greater part of the vacancies being filled by a particularly foul gang of Russians from Novo Georgiesk. They were Bolsheviki to a man, and the few good Russians of the old regular army who were already in the camp were quite unable to control them in any way. When my time was nearly up—my conduct had been quite exemplary—the Magdeburg Command began to pursue me with variations of all the trumped-up charges which they had tried to fake up while I was in the Kriegsgarnisonarrestanstalt. These charges had to be newly investigated by the military lawyers of Küstrin and tried by courts martial which sat in Berlin. The whole process dragged out for thirteen months. I was convicted every time—to this day I don't know what half the charges were—and sentenced to terms varying from three months to a year. I always appealed and once had a really comic re-trial, which I will try to describe later, by a superior court composed of fourteen perfectly serious generals and colonels.

Some kind of convention had been signed by the principal belligerents by which sentences awarded for offences against discipline only or directly connected with attempts to escape, if they exceeded fourteen days exclusive of time done awaiting trial, were to be postponed until the end of the war. There were many exceptions, and it was Magdeburg's game to get me on some charge which did not come under the terms of the convention.

All through the summer and autumn of 1917 we, at Küstrin, were hearing of successful escapes from the new camps in the Hanover district. As most of us were early prisoners who by our experiences and failures had gathered the information which contributed so largely to these successes and were now securely locked up in an unbreakable prison, we received the news with rather mixed feelings.

Fort Zorndorf is riddled with unfinished tunnels. One of them, of British manufacture, was over a hundred yards long and reached half-way across the ditch. It was given away to the Commandant by a Russian officer who had been soundly thrashed by one of the miners for stealing food—or so I was told, for the tunnel was discovered some time before I reached the camp. If the story is true, as I believe it to be, it is no reflection on the old Russian army, for the Russians at Küstrin were nearly all of the kind to which I have referred earlier in this chapter. The other tunnels had all been abandoned for one reason or another before I reached the camp.

It was well known among the British that there were two or more tunnels which led from the fort to outworks or observation posts several hundred yards away, and the entrance to one of them, in the part of the fort occupied by the guard and cut off from us, was definitely located. I met Trettner, the Commandant, in Berlin four years later, and he assured me that as far as he knew no such tunnels existed. Gaskell, of the Indian Army, with whom I shared a small living-hole under the main earthwork, joined with May, Fryer, Chichester-Constable, Grey, Wilkin, Hardy, myself and one or two others in an attempt to run a burrow into this tunnel.

There was in our part of the fort a pair of ventilators which apparently ventilated nothing, and we assumed that the communication tunnel was somewhere below them. We cut a hole in the floor of one of the rooms, under the iron sheet which stood before the door of the stove and covered the hole at all times except when workers were passing in or out, sunk a well about five feet deep and burrowed in the direction of the ventilators twenty yards away. We intended either to follow the ventilator shafts down to the roof of the tunnel, which must be some ten feet deep at this point or it would not clear the bed of the ditch, or, failing this, to burrow towards the known entrance and break in where the roof was nearer to the surface. The digging was very easy, the soil being pure sand, but the roof of the burrow had to be supported all the way, and almost every scrap of woodwork in the fort had been used up in earlier tunnels or burnt during the past severe winter. We worked to within a couple of feet of the ventilators, but came up against the solid blocks of granite which formed the foundations of the buildings above. The burrow had been very difficult to ventilate—there were two turns in it—and towards the end it was only possible for one man to work in it at a time, the sand being pulled out in a basin by two cords by which it was dragged backwards and forwards; even then the air became so foul that our candles would not burn for very long. This difficulty, added to the fact that we had used up the last remaining spaces under the floors and could find nowhere else to pack the excavated sand (the Russian mob being too untrustworthy for us to risk carrying it beyond the British quarters) caused us to give up this, the last possible hope of breaking out of Fort Zorndorf.

I have mentioned this tunnel not because, as a tunnel, it is particularly worthy of mention but because it is the only one in which I ever worked.

Between November 1917 and April 1918 I made five one-day excursions to Berlin to be tried by courts martial. Then there was some hitch which I never understood. I was still periodically examined on 'Protocols' from Magdeburg but never again came before a court.

I have explained before that it is quite possible to do a train journey in Germany, even a long one lasting two or three days, without ever speaking except to ask for a ticket—and two words, the class and the name of the place, are enough for that. Provided that the train was not 'visited' (in which case one had to show an identity card to the detectives, who knew a little more about identity papers than the Landsturm men of Neu Bruchausen) one ought, with ordinary luck, to have got through if one did not try to go too close to a frontier. One could always pretend to read a newspaper or sleep and treat conversationally inclined travellers to a grunt and a cloud of foul cigar smoke after the manner of a certain type of Hun. On my first three trips to Berlin, therefore, I was fully prepared to do a bolt and quick change if a chance should offer.

I used to wear my uniform with a white celluloid collar in place of the more usual drab flannel one and a pair of the worst kind of American yellow shoes with lumpy toes. Instead of socks I wore stockings under my trousers. I carried over my arm a Burberry with a goat-skin lining, folded to show only the lining so that it looked like a goat-skin coat. I carried a small hand-bag with some potted meat, chocolate and biscuits and a thermos flask full of coffee. I had to be away all day so this proceeding aroused no suspicion. Under my clothes, next to my skin, I carried a soft felt hat and a compass. A book which I took, ostensibly to read in the train, had a map of the Dutch frontier in one cover and a hundred marks in the other. The German searcher always looked down the back of a book, but had not yet arrived at examining the covers. I carried scissors. I had a pair of large round spectacles and some very foul cigars in my pockets. I was always searched before leaving the fort, but was not actually stripped. I wore as usual a long and straggling moustache.

The first time I was escorted by two junior N.C.O.'s who, beyond telling me how much they would enjoy shooting me if I would only give them a decent excuse, had nothing to say to me. I was hurried from the train to the court and back again and never had even the beginning of a chance.

On the second trip matters looked much more hopeful. On that occasion I was taken over from the camp guard by a sergeant-major and a private of the local infantry regiment, neither of whom had ever seen me before. The court martial was over by 12.30. On our way to the station the sergeant-major asked me if I would mind staying in Berlin until 7.30 p.m. His wife lived there and he wanted to see her and he could easily say we had missed the earlier train. I said I should be charmed.

He telephoned for the lady and, while we waited for her in a secluded corner of the third-class refreshment room, he confessed to a fondness for liquor, which was now, unfortunately, too expensive for him. I bought him a drink and gave the private one also, and after that they had another and then another. Then the lady arrived and we all had another. I was able to get rid of most of my share behind a radiator. With four glasses of German 'Kognak' inside him, the sergeant-major began to think the whole business of prisoner and escort rather rot and suggested a trip to the Zoo. I agreed and off we went. On the way I remarked to the private how nice it would be if he too could find a lady friend. He replied that he had two sisters in Berlin and asked the sergeant-major if he might telephone to them. The sergeant-major replied that he was a liar, but he could ring up all the ladies in Berlin if he liked, and he did not want to see him again until five minutes before the train started. That disposed of the private.

The gatekeeper at the Zoo objected strongly to my coming in, but was shouted down by the sergeant-major. We spent about two hours there—most of the animals seemed to have been eaten, but there was a golden pheasant still alive and a couple of very mangy monkeys—and visited the bar, where the sergeant-major had another couple, while his lady and I toyed with something light, but, although he was beginning to show many signs of alcoholic sloppiness, he never left my side.

After dark we wandered from one café to another. We were often refused admission on my account, but once I was taken to be a Bulgarian officer and a round of free drinks, in honour of this rather rare kind of ally, resulted.

By 7 p.m. we were back at the station, and

although it seemed to me that both the sergeant-major and his wife were very nearly full and were not apparently taking the least trouble to watch me they had managed to give me not the smallest possible chance to bring off the 'quick-change' for which I was so thoroughly prepared. One gleam of hope I had had when we passed a large public lavatory, but on my bolting into it with a hasty apology, the sergeant-major had followed me in and stood leaning against the door of my compartment until I emerged again.

The third trip again looked promising. This time we really did miss the train, and by a curious coincidence the N.C.O. of my escort, a middle-aged sergeant, again had a wife in Berlin. We had about two hours to wait and so walked out to find the lady, and again I had no difficulty in getting rid of the private in exactly the same way as on the last occasion. Again the sergeant had a taste for liquor and again I was able to oblige both him and his wife, but time was short and I could not get them much beyond the happily garrulous stage.

Returning to the station we passed that same large public lavatory that I had visited unsuccessfully the time before. More or less in desperation I apologised and darted in, the sergeant close on my heels. I opened a compartment near the entrance, the sergeant looked in, saw that there was no window and turned back to join his wife. I ran along the hall and went into about the tenth compartment from the one at which he had left me.

A WASTED PENNY

Now the sergeant had seen an English officer—rather oddly dressed but he didn't know that—in uniform, carrying a fur coat and wearing a long, drooping moustache, go into a compartment near the door. Two minutes later a perfectly good Hun, wearing a green felt hat, a waterproof, stockings, enormous spectacles and a hogged moustache and smoking a very foul cigar, walked out of a compartment at the other end of the hall. There seemed to be no reason why a rather fuddled sergeant should connect the two, and I hoped to walk out into the street with no more than a glance from him, but, instead of that, I opened my compartment and tripped out straight into his arms. So my penny was wasted.

The sergeant merely hiccoughed, '*Das geht nicht, Herr Hauptmann*' ('Nothing doing, Captain'), and helped me to re-disguise myself as a respectable prisoner of war. It seems that his wife, with truly Teutonic lack of false modesty, had wandered in behind us, had seen my change of compartments and had put her man on his guard.

He took it very well. Having led me on a pub-crawl round Berlin he dared make no report, and just as our train reached Küstrin he gave me back my green hat and said that, if I would keep quiet about how we had spent the day, he would too, adding that he was a soldier, he was, and no—— —— policeman.

He was a good fellow and I should have been very sorry to get him into trouble, but he had heard my criminal record enlarged upon by a fanatical prosecutor at the trial so would have had no one but himself to blame if he had lost me.

At this distance my attempt may seem to have been impossible of success and rather absurd, but it was an almost exact copy of the trick by which my good friend Terlinden, the Belgian, had escaped from a Berlin railway station—except that he had a beard to shave off.

I cannot leave Küstrin without giving some account of German military justice as I met it in Berlin.

The procedure followed at courts martial was, I believe, much the same as in other continental countries. The real trial took place before the officer who acted as *juge d'instruction* and whose business it was to secure a confession or something that could be argued to be a confession and to take from the witnesses statements, in his words, not theirs, which covered the facts as he imagined them to be.

The object of the court seemed to be always to record a conviction and sentence without delaying lunch, and without the slightest pretence of giving the prisoner a hearing even when he was represented by an advocate. Generally he was convicted 'on his own confession,' but, as I have explained, I spoilt all my 'confessions' by signing them as not understood. I was always convicted, therefore, on the strength of the prosecutor's harangue, which I could not follow very clearly, and the reading of a report from the Camp Commandant (the only evidence) at the scene of the alleged crime. I was always given an interpreter, but he wasn't allowed to interpret anything, and I never found out what he was for. Once, just before conviction, the President asked me, through a member of the court who spoke English well, whether I was satisfied with my trial. I began to say that I hadn't the foggiest idea what it was all about when the President rose and himself said very slowly and distinctly 'You are bloddy liar, mister,' (Laughter) whereupon the court retired to consider its finding and sentence.

I have mentioned that once I came before a military court of appeal and was actually acquitted—although certainly found guilty.

This court, instead of the five or six captains and majors of the lower courts, was composed of no less than fourteen aged and extremely pompous generals and colonels. They sat in a regular court-house with a crucifix over the President's head. I forget (if I ever knew) what the charges were and on what grounds I was appealing. We were encouraged to appeal but did not as a rule do so because it was odds on the prosecutor winning and getting the sentence doubled, but I had appealed for the sake of the trip to Berlin.

The procedure was much the same as in the lower courts, but the prosecutor got higher wages and brought off a much better frenzy. I employed an advocate, but he wasn't allowed to speak or perhaps he didn't want to. The Dutch Minister was present. Up to the moment of the 'withdrawal for deliberation' farce no one had taken any notice of me except the President, who had told me to take my hands out of my pockets. Then, as the court rose grunting to its feet, Trettner, the Zorndorf Commandant—of whom more later—stepped forward, handed up a paper and said a few words to the President. They all sat down again, the paper was passed round and there was a lot of hoarse whispering. Then the whole fourteen climbed again to their feet and, with the hot tears welling from their eyes, bowed solemnly and smiled at me not once but many times. Finally the President addressed me: 'You are convict,' he said; 'yes, you don it, yes, bot you are ackveet. No? Komplimente! Yes?' I asked the interpreter what he thought the old gent meant. 'Hell, that old guy's bughouse!' was the only answer I got, and I concluded that my appeal had succeeded. The prosecutor went in off the deep end, but the court retired without listening to him and I was marched out.

The explanation came when I was back in Zorndorf and asked Trettner what was the mysterious document which he had put in and which had apparently achieved the impossible. He handed me a copy of the daily orders of the General Officer Commanding, Küstrin District, of which one paragraph read something like this:

'I praise the English prisoner Hauptmann Cartwright who by his presence of mind and gallantry the valuable life of the German girl-child Anna Schütz who through the ice fallen had and but for his heroic rescue died have would regardless of the to him grave personal risk save did.'

Some weeks before, while skating on the flooded Oder marshes with a party of British officers (on parole) and one of the camp officers (who was a local ironmonger in better times—hence the permission to skate and an unlimited supply of inferior skates at superior prices) I had heard what I thought was a pig being killed. Going to investigate I had found the hideous face of a small girl sticking out of a hole in the ice, blowing bubbles and making the noise which had attracted me. The child was only a few yards from the bank and in a flooded meadow, which it was perfectly obvious could not have more than a couple of feet of water over it. As I approached, a small group of villagers and soldiers, who had collected on the bank, yelled at me to go back, shouting that the ice was thin, the water very deep and it was dangerous to get wet or something of the sort. I picked the little beast out and gave it to its screaming mother, who tried to kiss me. I did not get wet up to the middle.

I believe that Trettner (who was far too white a man to play the Magdeburg game) had faked up a report to the general, only with the ultimate object of using it at one of my trials. He confessed to the extreme view that a prisoner of war was entitled to a fair trial, and I suppose he felt that, a fair trial not being available, he was justified in using any means to defeat the prosecution.

Before concluding this chapter I must say a few words about this same Trettner.

The officers in charge of officers' camps were, as far as my experience went, a rather inferior lot. After the first few months, when nothing was left undone which could be done to make the prisoners' life unpleasant, most of them were content to let us alone as long as we kept quiet, and a very few tried actively to make life in the camps a little less unpleasant than the higher authorities intended it to be. The last were generally men who had seen fighting and were recovering from wounds or sickness; the others, various kinds of reservist who had no intention of ever going to any front. There were certain unspeakable swine about whom much was heard in the early days after the Armistice, but I never met any of them.

Reserve Captain Trettner was a thing apart. He was a genuine Prussian and had not travelled abroad or mixed with foreigners. He was enormously fat, and his face was heavily scarred by duelling in his student days. He was a perfectly white man. His camp, Fort Zorndorf, was a hole in the ground and nothing could make it fit for prolonged habitation, but anything which it was possible to do to better the lot of his prisoners he did willingly and generally without being asked. I can only give a few examples.

Walks, on parole, were an institution (by international agreement) when I arrived at Zorndorf; but, whereas in the Magdeburg district the prisoners were formed into crocodiles, like girls' schools, and marched out with an ostentatiously armed under-officer at each end, at Zorndorf we were sent out with an unarmed and (perhaps protestingly) well-behaved officer, who merely showed us the way and kept the time. Instead of once or twice a week we went out every day.

Trettner lived in a cottage just outside the fort and three or four officers were invited there every day to read the papers, sit in the garden, play bridge or chess or walk in the woods with him. It wasn't everybody's idea of enjoying life but it was so obviously well meant that it was difficult to refuse. There was nothing on earth to prevent one from bolting on these occasions, but we were so obviously trusted that we had to admit to a sort of implied parole. Three of the first Englishmen at Zorndorf, not knowing Trettner's intentions, were summoned by an under-officer to the presence one day soon after they arrived. The under-officer wore the usual pistol. They saw only that they were to be taken outside the camp—which meant the possibility of a bolt. They had reversible coats, etc., and were ready at any time to mobilise in five minutes. They kept the under-officer waiting five minutes and mobilised. As soon as they were clear of the guard and in the wood they bolted. They were caught but Trettner never quite got over it;

he simply could not see their point of view and regarded their bolting as the blackest treachery. Some of us used to argue with him for hours at a time to try to make him understand that those three had been absolutely justified, morally and actually, in bolting and that we considered ourselves free to escape at any time when we had not deliberately given our parole, and that some of us even thought we were justified in considering our parole automatically cancelled when, after giving it, we were insulted by being kept under an armed guard—as was done in some camps. He said it was a simple matter of honour and never would ask for the parole of anyone who went to his house.

When I was left alone at Zorndorf with the Russian riff-raff Trettner gave me a small room to myself and found a decent Russian peasant to act as servant to me. He put a lock on the door and even offered me the services of a German sentry to guard me! This last was because I had assisted in a mix-up with a gang of Russians whom we had caught trying to steal food from one of the British rooms, and his interpreter had told him that some of them had vowed vengeance. It had not been a very fierce business, but had made a lot of noise, and two of us had had to be treated for Russky bites. Perhaps I ought to have accepted his offer and thereby deprived the Fatherland of one more defender.

The first week or two that I was alone Trettner sent me out for parole walks with an under-officer, or soldier—quite decent men, but I got a little sick of their conversation. He came to the conclusion that my life alone with the Russians was unliveable, and after making himself thoroughly unpopular with the higher authorities eventually wrested from them permission for me to go out alone. He wrote out a card which I signed and which was kept in the camp office. I only had to go in at one door of the office, take the card and walk out of the other door and out of the fort. I was on parole until I brought the card back. It was summer and I could be out from 9 a.m. to 8 p.m. and could go anywhere except into the town of Küstrin. I was nominally in uniform but mostly wore a shirt and grey flannel trousers and attracted very little attention. It was a pleasant country of lakes and pine woods and I spent many hours bathing. The Russians made a great outcry about it, and finally the same privilege was extended to about half a dozen of them. The first time out they made a bee-line for the nearest village, got drunk and went for the women and that (as had been foreseen) was the end of their unescorted walks.

Foreign newspapers of all sorts (except the *Continental Times*, edited by Trebitsch Lincoln, and a few German propaganda rags published in Switzerland) were strictly forbidden by Berlin. Trettner used to go frequently to Berlin and always brought back a *Times*, which anyone who went to his house could read. When I was alone he obtained it daily through his bank and used to bring it to my room himself nearly every morning. The copies were only four or five days old and uncensored. I cannot describe what this meant to me after seeing only German newspapers for more than three years.

Trettner attended several of my trials and always made one or more protests against the advantage which was taken of my ignorance of the procedure of the courts. On one occasion I travelled back to Küstrin in the train with him, when, in spite of angry protests from the officers who made up the bulk of the first-class travellers, he gave me dinner in the restaurant car.

Some time in 1917 the last bottle of Scotch whisky was auctioned at the officers' club in Küstrin. Trettner bought it. He sent for Gaskell and me, who happened to be the two senior prisoners in the camp, and sold us the bottle for two cakes of soap. (Real soap was practically unobtainable in Germany after the end of 1915.)

When I left Küstrin for Schweidnitz, Trettner came to the station to see me off. He told my escort the 'Anna Schütz' story and ordered them to treat me with great respect. As the train left he called out to me in German to write and tell him if I had any trouble on the journey. This was why, when my escort applied at Liegnitz for accommodation for the night, and were told to dump me in the cells, they firmly protested and I was grudgingly given a bed in a barrack-room.

If I have wandered too far from my story it is no further than Trettner stands out in my mind above all the other Germans whom I met in nearly four years of captivity.

In the first week of January 1918 I was suddenly warned for a move, in twenty-four hours, to an unknown destination. A tame clerk told me that I was going to Aachen (Aix la Chapelle). I thought this might mean that I should be offered exchange to Holland, of which there had been a lot of talk in the newspapers but I knew that it meant a very fine chance to escape, since Aachen is only four or five miles from the Dutch frontier. The next day I was told that my move was off, Magdeburg having whipped up another charge for trial. A few days later another British officer was sent to Aachen. He went fully prepared to escape, but other officers there persuaded him not to try so he refused the exchange when it was offered and came back to Zorndorf. Then another officer was sent to Aachen, escaped from the camp and was recaptured at the frontier. After this all officers of known 'bad character' had to sign a statement to the effect that they wished to be exchanged—which would amount, morally, to a parole—before they were allowed to leave Küstrin for Aachen.

I was told that my sentences and all charges pending against me would be washed out if I would write a letter applying for exchange. I replied—and put it in writing to the Commandant—that I did not wish to be exchanged, and that as long as I was in Germany and under guard I should consider myself free to escape. I was most completely equipped and was perfectly confident that if only I could get away from that infernal fort I should be able to get clear of the Fatherland, no matter what the distance to a frontier. By the end of January I was the only British officer left at Zorndorf, and I remained there alone among that mob of unsavoury Russians until June, when I was joined by two newly torpedoed officers of the Merchant Service.

SCHWEIDNITZ

On 18th July I was moved to Schweidnitz, in Silesia, arriving there on the 20th. I spent the intervening night in a crowded barrack-room of the local regiment at Liegnitz. The twenty or thirty men who slept in the room were all—recruits and old soldiers alike—ripe for mutiny. I wondered if their officers knew about it.

I was now near the end of my fourth year of imprisonment and I was two hundred kilometres farther from any neutral frontier than I had ever been before.

I had, however, lately acquired a very perfect forgery of a German working man's 'identity card' properly printed and stamped and with my description, trade (locksmith), military category, etc., filled in in German script. In the margin was a certified photograph of myself in working clothes. With this card in my possession I had every hope of being able to do a long railway journey if I could only find a way out of the camp.

During my thirteen months at Zorndorf I had collected many good maps and all manner of other useful stores, all of which were very securely hidden, and I was probably by far the best equipped prisoner in Germany. I still had about one hundred marks, Zorndorf being the only camp in Germany at which prisoners were still allowed to have real money.

Schweidnitz was a very difficult camp to get out of.

There had been two very obvious exits, but both had been used—and therefore sealed up—shortly before my arrival. One, a short tunnel, had been used by a number of prisoners (there were none but Englishmen in the camp) who got out one night and walked over the frontier into Bohemia, not, I was told, with any great hope of getting home but to finish their time in the hands of the Austrians, who were known to treat their prisoners very much better than the Germans.* The other had been used by the 'maniac' Hardy, who, with Loder-Symonds, had gone all the way to the Dutch frontier by train and got clear away.

The only possible way out that I could find was over the barbed wire at one particular point where it was under the observation of a single sentry who patrolled outside it. He had, to cover him in bad weather, an open-sided box which was perched on a scaffolding over the middle of the fence which he had to watch. From his box he could see the fence

* See note on page 302.

on either side of it, but he most certainly could not see through its floor. I thought it might be possible, in a heavy downpour of rain, which would drive the sentry into the box and so drum on its tin roof as to deafen him to all ordinary noises, to get over the fence under the box and away down a slope which fell sharply from the fence without coming into his view at all.

I had been dumped on arrival into the company of two Englishmen who had been considering the possibility of escape in general and had given some attention to this particular line. We decided to try it. They had their own plans for reaching a frontier (which involved, I believe, fraternising with the disloyal Czech element in Bohemia), and I intended to try a lone train journey, counting on my identity card to get me through all difficulties until I should come to the frontier zone.

The fence which we had to negotiate was about eight feet high, and we had to make somehow a sectional or telescopic ladder which could be carried unseen to a porch within a few feet of the sentry-box and there quickly put together at the very last moment. Cutting the wire, instead of going over it, was out of the question. The only wire-cutters at our disposal would have taken much too long for a job which could only succeed if carried out in a few seconds and without any sort of hitch.

In one of the large rooms in which the prisoners lived and which had been the kitchen of something equivalent to a workhouse, there were a number of large cooking ranges of the continental pattern. These were surrounded by a kind of grid which when removed from the ranges, proved to be excellent ready-made sections of a light steel ladder. We only had to cut them to the right length and make some kind of clips to fasten the sections together. I had plenty of hacksaw blades, and we made quite satisfactory clips from stout wire taken from some of the internal fittings of the ovens. The finished article would be a light but perfectly rigid steel ladder about nine feet long in three easily assembled sections.

A fortnight after my arrival in Schweidnitz the ladder was nearly ready when the Commandant, who was, I think, a Pole, paid a friendly visit (he was on quite good terms with most of the prisoners) to the box—formerly porter's lodge—in which I took my meals with the other two and in which they also slept.

In the course of conversation he mentioned that he very much hoped that none of us would be so foolish as to attempt to escape. In the first place, escape at that distance from a frontier was quite impossible except to a man who knew the language perfectly and could pass as a German, and who must be, moreover, provided with a number of papers which it was quite impossible for a prisoner to obtain. Secondly, or more properly firstly, an order had come from the War Ministry to the effect that the Commandant and officers of any camp which lost a prisoner—temporarily or permanently—

would be sent forthwith to the west front, without regard to their age or medical category.

I made some excuse, connected with my cash account, to inquire whether my dossier had arrived from Küstrin. The Commandant replied that he thought it had come but he had not yet had time to look at it. This conversation took place just before 'lights out,' and I think he must have gone straight to the *Kommandantur* and read it, or part of it, after which he must have done some hectic telephoning to a higher authority.

Anyhow he did me the honour of attending at my bedside before 'reveille' the next morning. With tears in his eyes he told me that he was shocked and horrified to find that I had been a prisoner for nearly four years; he could not understand by what slackness in high places those not very nice Prussians of Magdeburg had been allowed so long to delay my exchange. I was to pack up immediately and proceed to Aachen by the 11 something train. He asked no question and made no suggestion that I should sign anything.

AACHEN

I left Schweidnitz on the first of August and arrived at Aachen on the 3rd, having spent the two intervening nights in the train.

On the journey I was fully equipped for a four or five days' walk and had, moreover, the same properties for a quick change as I had had when I tried that game in Berlin except that, instead of a service dress suit, I wore the specially made blue uniform which I shall describe later. I should have every chance of success if I could only get away from my escort, at no matter what distance from the frontier, either by day or by night.

My escort consisted of two young and rather stupid-looking infantrymen, one of them a lance-corporal. As soon as we were in the train they put their rifles in the rack, took off their boots and made themselves as comfortable as the wooden seats of a German third-class carriage permit. I had every hope of them. We changed several times before reaching Berlin, but my escort told me that from there we should get a through train to Aachen. I hoped to be able to slip them during the second night of the journey, when we should be somewhere in Westphalia. I have met half a dozen men who had slipped their escorts during night journeys, or had seen others do it, and I had ready-made plans to meet any likely situation. My stupid-looking escort defeated all my plans by the simple expedient of sleeping all day, one on each side of me, with their belts buckled together across my stomach and hooked into their pack-braces. There were always one or two other people in the carriage, otherwise probably I could have cut or unbuckled the belts and walked out without waking them, so soundly did they sleep. When I went to the lavatory compartment and looked out of the window I found myself looking into the smiling face of one of them who was leaning from the next window and tickling my chin with the muzzle of his rifle. The other had of course escorted me and was standing guard outside the door. Having slept all day they spent the night—the whole of it, there was no slacking—either standing or sitting on their packs with their backs to the two doors of the compartment.

So I arrived at Aachen about midday on 3rd August.

The first prisoner I saw in the camp was my good friend Antony, an Australian whom I had known at Küstrin in 1917. He told me that he had been there for some six weeks with a large party of officers and N.C.O.'s whose exchange had been held up on account of some squabble between the Germans and the Dutch, the latter being accused of taking more Englishmen than Germans into the country. Before going to Aachen for exchange Antony had made one or more attempts to escape, and, by way of a hobby, he had made a thorough study of the camp during the six weeks in which he had been held up in it. At first sight the place seemed very secure, but Antony was able to show me immediately how I could get out of it if the necessary apparatus—forty-two feet of rope stout enough to bear my weight—could be got together. I decided to have one night in bed to get rid of some of the soreness resulting from forty-eight hours of bumping on a wooden seat and to try my luck the next night.

Antony assured me that the scoffers were all in Holland and that I could count, if necessary, on the help of every prisoner in the camp.

We were kept in a high, oblong building of four stories which had been some kind of technical school. It was surrounded by a small garden, a part of which had been wired in to form an exercise ground, the fence round the rest of it consisting of a dwarf wall surmounted by high ornamental spiked railings. A few strands of barbed wire had been interwoven through the railings—they would give me a foothold but could serve no other useful purpose. The prisoners were hunted in and shut up at dusk, after which there were, as far as we knew, four sentries on the outside of the building—two to each long side, their beats extending round the short sides. There were about half a dozen sentries posted inside the building during the night. Another sentry was known to be posted under a railway bridge just outside the camp, but he did not seem to be found by the camp guard and he appeared to be more concerned with the bridge than with the camp.

Antony had arranged for an Australian N.C.O. to help him to lower me from the window of a room on the second floor into some shrubs which grew between the short side of the building and the garden fence. Outside the fence was a wide street carrying a fair amount of traffic.

I only regret that I have no record of the name of this N.C.O. who gave me such valuable assistance, or of any of the other prisoners who helped in various ways. I knew them only for a few hours.

The first thing to be done was to get hold of the necessary rope. We found in a large lecture-room, not occupied by prisoners, a big electric lamp which could be raised or lowered by a wire cable passing through a pulley in the ceiling. We made a staging of tables, beds and chairs, and after tying the lamp to the pulley with an assortment of bits of string, cut the cable. This gave us about thirty of the forty-two feet which we reckoned would be required. Some odds and ends of clothes-line from the exercise ground, twisted together with string, gave another seven feet, and a sheet completed the job.

The room in which Antony and I slept was on the floor above the room from which I was to be lowered, and after 9.30 p.m. a sentry was posted on the stairs to prevent anyone from going up or down. At 10 p.m. the prisoners were counted in bed.

At about 9 p.m. on the 4th August Antony and I went into cover behind some odds and ends of furniture in the empty lecture-room which was on the second floor—the floor from which I was to be lowered. Dummies, their scalps made from fur flying-gloves, occupied our beds on the floor above.

I was wearing a blue uniform which had been specially designed by my wife in Minehead. The jacket was cut more like the coat of a lounge suit than the jumper it was supposed to represent. It had all the usual shoulder-straps, stars, pocket-flaps and brass buttons. The trousers had the usual red stripe. It had completely deceived the censors at Küstrin, who would have cut lengths out of the sleeves and legs and let in material of another colour had they not believed it to be a perfectly normal uniform. I wore a celluloid collar and carried a uniform cap of the 'gorblimey' type minus the badge, strap and stuffing. I had two compasses about me and what I believed to be a very fine map of the district. The map was the one on which Terlinden had escaped; he had smuggled it back to me with his route, which I did not intend to follow, marked on it.

I had two or three small pieces of chocolate and a few biscuits in my pockets, my main food supply —I needed only enough for twenty-four hours— being in the pockets of my Burberry which was tied up *en banderole* and waiting for me in the room from which I was to be lowered. The roll was to be slipped over my head as soon as I was through the window and in position to be let down.

Soon after 10 p.m. some taps on the floor above told us that our dummies had passed the inspection and we heard the German staff retire to their quarters a few minutes later.

I converted my uniform into civilian clothing by ripping off all the stars, flaps, etc., and Antony and I went into the other room, where the rope was already in position with one end tied to a radiator. I took up my position astride the window-sill, with one foot through a loop in the end of the wire rope.

It was very dark and raining hard. I didn't trust the rope, I have no very good head for heights, and at that moment I hated everything. At 10.45 Antony, who had gone to watch from a window at the front of the building, came in and reported that the sentry on that side was moving towards the middle of the building (i.e. at the end of his beat farthest from the spot, on the short side of the building, where I should land). A moment later the Australian N.C.O., who had been watching at the back, came in and reported that his sentry was in a corresponding position. The two of them then took the rope to lower me down.

The N.C.O.'s who occupied the room (no officers lived in it) had remained in bed and kept absolute silence, as they had been told to, up to this point, but now they crowded round the window all wanting to lend a hand on the rope. The result was that the man who was to have slipped my Burberry over my head was crowded out. I forgot all about him and it, and told the others to lower away as soon as I was clear of the window-sill. As it turned out I got in such a sweat hurrying through that hot night that I should have discarded the Burberry very soon, but I should have been glad of the extra food in its pockets.

Before I was lowered we had noticed a glimmer of light which we thought came from a grating covering a window in a basement below the level of the ground on which I should land. As soon as I was at the limit of the rope, which left me about two feet from the ground, I discovered that the light instead of coming from below ground came from the window of the guard-room on the ground floor and that I was hanging right in front of it with what light there was full on me. To make matters worse before I could steady myself I had swung with both feet against the window. Although the rain was making a great rattling on the bushes the crash which I made must have sounded quite loudly in the room, but the guard, who were gambling round a table at the far end of it, took no particular notice; one or two of them looked round but saw nothing but the very dirty panes of glass.

I was on the point of dropping to the ground when a sentry, of whose existence we had not known, suddenly came to life among the bushes within a few feet of me and strolled away round the corner of the building. He must have had his back towards me, but how on earth he managed not to hear me I cannot imagine, for it had seemed to me as I was being lowered that the wire scraping over the stone window-sill was making a noise like a double bass in full blast. Probably he was dozing and never knew what woke him up. I heard afterwards that a cushion which was placed under the wire to deaden the sound was cut in half by the first two or three feet of it.

When the sentry had disappeared I dropped to the ground and crawled away through the bushes to the railings. It took me nearly half an hour to get over them. It was not an easy climb, and I had to do it silently. Half a dozen times I was nearly over but had to drop back because people were passing in the road outside, or I heard sentries coming my way, but I was perfectly safe in the darkness of the bushes in the intervals.

It was 11.15 p.m. when I looked at my watch after passing—reeling slightly—the sentry under the bridge, who took no notice of me, and I knew that I should have my work cut out to do the walk which I had planned before dawn. I went straight into the town which, thanks to the attentions of our bombing planes, was in total darkness.

Aachen is only four or five kilometres from the frontier, but, owing to the large number of sons of the Fatherland who had deserted and crossed to Holland in the neighbourhood, the line thereabouts was very closely guarded and in some places wired. I believe that the rumour of live wires along the frontier was quite unfounded, though they were certainly used between Holland and Belgium.

In view of the difficulty of crossing near the town I had decided to go about twenty-four kilometres (fifteen miles) in a north-westerly direction the first night, lie up for one day and cross in open country the next night. My map showed a large wood, more than one kilometre square, at about the right distance and I hoped to find good cover in it for the lie-up. A railway was shown running through the southern end of the wood, and, if I kept to the north of that and went roughly west from the wood, I must strike the frontier within from four to six kilometres. Hereabouts the frontier was clearly defined by a small stream which I thought would be easy to find and identify because there was a main line of railway running parallel and close to it on the German side. Even more important than an easily identified frontier was a clearly defined sentry line, and this was provided here in its easiest form. I knew that the railway was the closely guarded line, with sentries at short intervals along it, and that the stream was watched by only a few men with long beats. There would be dogs, but they would be probably with the men on the railway.

There are two roads which run roughly north-east from Aachen and they leave the town within a few hundred yards of one another but separate once they are clear of the suburbs. I knew that the more westerly of the two—the one nearer the frontier—was patrolled, and I intended, therefore, to follow the more easterly one. To get on to my road I had only to find a main street running more or less north and south (it was shown clearly on my map) and follow it until my road branched from it.

I found the street and followed it without any loss of time, the clouds having parted for long enough to show the pole-star so that I did not have to look at the compass.

Then somehow I went wrong and was following what I thought was my road at top speed, when suddenly, two or three kilometres from the town, a patrol bobbed up from a ditch on my right and called on me to halt. There was an unfenced field of grass or stubble on my left and I bolted blindly into it. It was pitch dark and they made no attempt to follow me and did not even let off the customary useless fireworks.

After a rather difficult detour I came back to the road and was able to check my position on the map by means of a stream which flowed under a small culvert. I ought to have gone off across country in an easterly direction until I found the road which I had meant to take, but it was getting late, so I stuck to the one I was on until I came to a cross-road which led in the right direction. After my meeting with the patrol I took to the fields and lay doggo whenever I heard anyone approaching—and there were a surprising number of people about that night—and made detours round a couple of straggling hamlets.

I found the right road, which had, as the map showed, degenerated from a full-blown *chaussée* into a country road, but I came at once upon a long string of habitations and had to keep mostly to the fields and lanes parallel to it. It was often rather difficult going, but there was no real hitch until I was within four or five kilometres of my wood, when I came on long rows of electric lights which my map did not account for in any way. I wasted a lot of time studying it and trying to make out how I had gone wrong and where I had actually got to.

I had no torch (there were several hidden in my heavy baggage, but this had not arrived from Schweidnitz when I left Aachen) and only one box (there were several in my Burberry) of damp matches, and I had to lie down in standing corn before I dared strike them to look at the map. I think the lights marked some new coal-mines—that is to say, they were newer than my map, which may have been any age.

I failed completely to fix my position on the map and had to go on on a dead reckoning, trusting to be able to pick up my wood somehow at dawn. Then I wasted a lot more time trying to find a way through the lighted patch of country without going too near any of the lamps or running into any of the people whom I could see moving about. In the end I had to walk through it along a brightly lighted road between high boarded fences, but fortunately got to the darkness the other side without meeting anyone. While I was trying to find a way through the mines a dozen or more rifle shots were fired in one of the compounds. These, I gathered afterwards, were fired at a gang of Russian soldiers who were breaking out *en masse*. While in the lighted patch I crossed a railway which, if I ignored the mines, put me once more on terms with my map and I went on more hopefully. Almost immediately, however, I came on two more railway tracks of which there was no sign on the map, and I had to conclude once more that I was hopelessly lost. Again I had lost time, and, since dawn had broken and it was getting rapidly lighter, I rather hopelessly turned west to look for my wood where it ought to be if I had kept somewhere near the right line.

Almost at once I saw it ahead of me and a couple of kilometres distant, but before I could reach it nearly full daylight had come and at least three people saw me, wet through and a most obvious fugitive, hurrying through the standing crops. A year ago the nearest village would have turned out with dogs and beaten through the wood. Now those who saw me were too war-weary to care or perhaps thought me a deserter and, if so, wished me luck.

On studying the map carefully by daylight I came to the conclusion that I had made no mistake—except when I took the wrong road out of Aachen—and that all the features which had upset my calculations were, in fact, newer than the map.

I lay undisturbed in the wood all day. I was wet through and therefore cold, although it was a warm and fairly fine day. I had my few biscuits and bits of chocolate and had eaten a large meal before I left the camp, so that, although I could have done with the contents of my Burberry pockets, I was not excessively hungry. I had filled all my pockets with ears of wheat during the night and spent a great part of the day rubbing out and eating the grain, but this provided more occupation than sustenance.

I came out of the wood at about 9.30 p.m., but

it was still too light and a good many people were about so I got inside a corn stook and lay curled up there for about an hour, and very comfortable it was after lying in wet undergrowth all day.

At about 10.30 I started off on a compass bearing, my direction being a little north of west, but, as on the night before, I got on very slowly on account of the many new features which were not shown on my map. In attempting to check my position and in avoiding all places where there was a likelihood of encountering natives, I was forced to follow a line more and more to the north of my proper course. I well knew the danger of this and took a turn due south whenever I was able. The danger of travelling too far north lay in the fact that, two or three kilometres north of the point at which I aimed, the frontier turned westwards at right angles to the stream which I have mentioned above. If I crossed the railway and stream too far to the north I should therefore be still in Germany.

When I was within two or three kilometres of the frontier I had to pass a patch of very close country; the fences, which were often thick hedges with plenty of barbed wire in the weak places, held me up long and often. I tried not to use any kind of lane or enclosed track, for I knew that they were just the sort of defiles in which, in that close country, sentries would be posted; but about half an hour before I found the railway for which I was looking I was forced, by fences which I could not negotiate, into a narrow lane.

I was hardly in it when I saw a figure approaching me and dropped silently against the hedge-bottom on the right of the lane. The figure was coming on the left of the lane, and had it kept to that side would have passed without a possibility of seeing me. I could see against the sky that it was a soldier, and I had the impression that it was a very ancient one. Ten yards short of me he crossed over the lane to my side and would have walked almost on top of me. I had to jump up and meet him, and the meeting was not a success from his point of view. I had been carrying, all the evening, a stout fencing stake which I had picked up on the edge of the wood when I came out of it and I swung this, not kindly, as I jumped. Then I ran. What I did was probably the most foolish thing a prisoner could do, for the assaulted sentry might have raised all the guards for miles round, but I was within a short walk of the frontier, which I had been trying for more than three years to get across and the man's appearance was so sudden that I had no time to think.

I came out almost at once into open cornfields and settled down in the middle of one to review the situation.

It was getting late and I knew that I had no time to waste if I was to cross the railway and stream in full darkness. I knew also that I had come as far north as was safe and must watch the compass continually, no matter how much time I might lose thereby, to avoid crossing the stream beyond the angle of the frontier. I ought, if I was where I thought I was, to find the railway within about one kilometre. I was very thirsty, having had nothing to drink for more than twenty-four hours. Finally I had just added to the normal prisoner's desire to escape an excellent incentive to make no mistake this time. It was raining very heavily.

I came out of the corn and started off due west, and got a long drink from a puddle of fresh rain-water in the first track which I crossed. After a few hundred yards I saw a telegraph line against the sky in front of me and concluded that the railway ran beneath it. I stalked it cautiously and painfully on my stomach, only to find that the line crossed the middle of a cornfield and had no apparent connection with any railway.

After another quarter of a mile or so exactly the same thing happened again. Those two telegraph lines lost me, between them, not less than half an hour. I had not yet found the railway and the first signs of dawn were showing in the east.

I went on again and in a few minutes came to a very dense wood of closely planted fir trees. I went straight into the wood and crashed steeply downhill into what I knew must be the valley of my stream at last. I made a lot of noise, but in that downpour of rain no one was likely to hear me unless within a few yards of me. It was as dark as pitch in the wood and once or twice I burst into and across paths and rides—very dangerous spots—before I realised what they were. About ten minutes after entering the wood I heard the roar of a train in front of me and quite close and came almost at once to the top of a cutting through which the railway ran. After the darkness of the wood it seemed most alarmingly light and there was in fact very much more light than suited my purpose.

I lay down in some bushes at the top of the bank to listen for the coughs and other familiar night sounds of the German sentries, who were, I knew, posted on or near the railway. I had not waited many minutes when a number of rifle shots were fired in the woods somewhere behind me, and I heard men, presumably sentries, calling to one another up and down the railway in both directions. These shots were fired at a gang of Russians who, like those of the night before, had broken out of the mines and were running blindly towards the west. I saw three of them at the quarantine camp later in the day. About a dozen had broken out each time and several had been killed or wounded before they were through the wire of their compounds; the fate of the remainder was unknown, but the German had very little consideration for quite tame Russian soldiers and none for those who showed any sort of independence.

What I wanted to do was to locate two sentries definitely and then cross the line midway between them. After a time—and it was getting horribly lighter every minute—I saw a soldier coming along the line on my right, flashing an electric torch in the air, apparently as a signal to some one in the woods above the cutting. On my left I could hear voices, but could not make out the speakers through the bushes in which I lay. The torchbearer apparently met them—they were stationary—said a few words and started back the way he had come. At the same time I heard a dog whining and a man cursing it in the woods behind me, and decided that I had got to move without more delay.

Providentially I heard a train approaching at the very moment when I had got to my feet. I waited for it, ran down the side of the cutting as it came in sight and crossed the line under cover of its noise and smoke. I took a heavy toss over the first line of metals and a heavier one over the signal wires at the far side—they twanged like a hundred banjos —and flopped down in a bed of nettles at the top of the cutting without a challenge. I crawled to the edge of the nettles and found myself looking down on a wide and well-kept road along which at the moment a squad of weary soldiers was marching. I was worried, not by the soldiers, who could not possibly see me, but by the road which was where, according to my map, no road had any right to be. I got out the map and found to my relief that, if it showed no road running by the railway at the point where I thought I was, it showed none at any other point.

I could only conclude that the road, like the mines and the railways which had worried me the night before, was newer than the map, assume that I was on the right line after all, and go straight ahead.

I had not much of a view from my nettles—they were very vicious nettles!—but could see, about a hundred yards ahead and beyond a slight rise in the ground, a long row of poplars which I thought must mark the stream. It was by now broad daylight, and there was no sort of cover by which I could approach the stream. It was out of the question to wander about between the two guarded lines looking for a better approach, so I put my head down and sprinted for the poplars feeling much more conspicuous than I liked. At the foot of the poplars I found, instead of a stream, a wire fence over which I blundered and continued the sprint until I landed, fifty yards farther on, in a small wood.

As I ran into the wood I cleared a small boggy stream. My map told me only that there would be a small stream; it did not tell me whether it would be one or ten yards wide and I now rather unwisely assumed that I had crossed it and was in Holland. I went straight on through the wood, not at all cautiously, but the moment I got to the other side of it I saw, some seventy-five yards ahead, a double row of poplars with a gleam of water at their feet, and knew that here really was the frontier.

I could see no sentry, but there were groups of bushes all along the banks, any one of which might hide a man, so again I put down my head and sprinted for the nearest point of the stream. When I was ten yards from it a Landsturmer popped up on my left, bellowing 'Halt!' I jinked and took a header into the water. It took me seven strokes to cross and the German got his rifle off just as I got my hand on the far bank.

When I crawled out I knew I was in Holland.

PASSING THE POST

As soon as I was out of the water I ran as if the devil were after me for a hamlet which I could see a few hundred yards ahead. I approached a woman who was just opening her cottage, but she only screamed and banged the door in my face. Next I met a fat farmer on a bicycle whom I stopped and to whom I explained the situation in halting

German, asking him where I could find a soldier or policeman who would be good enough to arrest me, dry me, and feed me. He was quite friendly and said that if I kept straight on I should probably run into a patrol. At the first cross-road three Dutch soldiers jumped out of a ruined cottage with rifles at the ready and called 'Halt!' I told them I was an English officer, lately arrived from the Fatherland and in urgent need of food and dry clothing, and one of them conducted me to the guard-house in the village of Rimburg. There I ate all that remained of the guards' rations of the day before and changed into the uniform of a Dutch private soldier while my clothes were being dried. The guard-house was at a road post actually on the frontier, the barrier was just in front of it and on the other side of the barrier was a German sentry. I leant on the barrier and told the Hun my then unbiased opinion of him and his Fatherland and everything connected with it and gave him a note, in the worst possible taste, for the Commandant of the camp at Aachen.

When my clothes were dry an under-officer drove me some miles in a cab to a quarantine station, where exchanged British N.C.O.'s were disinfected on arrival from Germany. There I had a big meal, a shave and a bath and saw three of the Russian soldiers who had been the cause of the shooting the night before. The place seemed to be run by Englishwomen, who overwhelmed me with kindnesses.

In the evening a Dutch officer came and took me by train to Rotterdam, where we arrived at about 11 p.m. Unfortunately I had discarded my celluloid collar as soon as I was clear of the town of Aachen and had been unable to buy a new one at the quarantine camp, so, in my roughly dried blue suit, I looked a bit out of place in a first-class carriage. The officer took me to a good hotel and, after a few minutes talk with the porter, said: 'Your room is number so and so; I advise you to find your Consul-General to-morrow. You are free. Good night.

It felt more than a little odd—being free!

At the Consulate I was supplied with money and an outfit of clothing, etc., given a temporary passport and told that I had just missed a convoy and must wait about ten days for another.

The convoy, consisting of three small ships with an escort of about a dozen destroyers, left the Hook on the 15th August and I went ashore at Gravesend the next day.

On arrival at the War Office I was sent to report to half a dozen different departments, mostly minor ramifications of the Intelligence Department. Then I was given double the active service allowance of ration coupons and told to take three months' leave and get fat. Before my leave began I had the honour of being summoned to Windsor, where I was received in private by the King—and felt that all my efforts had not been quite in vain.

Early in September Harrison came home,

wounded, from France, and supported me at my wedding to the one to whom, above all others, my escape was due.

In the middle of September Major-General Sir Amyatt Hull, who had been my commanding officer at the outbreak of war, came home on short leave and I saw him in London. He offered to get me posted to a battalion in his division, and I knew then that I should have only myself to blame if I could not recover the ground which I had lost to my contemporaries during those four long, wasted years. He had no doubt that the war would last out the winter and advised me to make the most of my leave and get thoroughly fit. By the end of September the Germans were showing definite signs of cracking and when their allies began to fade out I went up to the War Office and asked to be allowed to cancel my leave and go to France. I was met with a blank refusal. I might go to any other front, but it had been decided that escaped prisoners could not be allowed to go back to the western front (although the three other maniacs got there) and risk recapture and possible severe punishment by the Germans. I think I knew as much as anyone at the W.O. about the Germans' treatment of recaptured prisoners, and it had never done me much harm. No other front was any use to me, so I started in to worry every one I could get at, and finally my importunities, coupled with a letter from General Hull to some one in authority, resulted in my being invited, towards the end of October, to sit down and scribble out a statement that I was going to France at my own request and would accept full responsibility for the result in the event of my again becoming a prisoner —that, apparently, was all they wanted!

I was promised immediate orders. I received them on the 5th November and steamed into Boulogne Harbour at 11 a.m. on the 11th November 1918, which, as all the world knows, was the exact moment of the 'Cease Fire.' So my efforts were wasted after all.

NOTE ON ESCAPES FROM SCHWEIDNITZ (page 276)

* Since the publication of the first edition I have met an old friend who was in Schweidnitz at the time of this attempt. He told me the names of the escapers, after which I needed no further assurance from him that the suggestion that they were out to better their lot by re-capture in Austria was quite false. Several of them were old friends of mine who had made numerous difficult attempts without ever giving a thought to their own comfort. Their plans in this case were perfectly workable and it was only by consistent bad luck that none of them succeeded. I had the story on hearsay and very much regret having repeated it.

VIII

CONCLUSION

By M. C. C. HARRISON

AFTER my return to England in September 1917 there is not much more for me to narrate.

My first thought was to take what steps I could to help my friends in Germany, by arranging for mobilisation stores to be sent out to those who were genuinely trying to escape. Needless to say I did not forget Cartwright, and when I met his fiancée, whose welcome parcels I had seen on many occasions in Germany, I gave her a complete list of everything that I considered might possibly be of assistance.

In December I re-joined my old regiment in France and found just one or two familiar faces in the Transport lines.

On the 21st March 1918 we were in the front line trenches of the Fifth Army and spent most of that day behind the German lines. A desperate counter-attack by the Connaught Rangers in the evening enabled me with the remnants of the battalion to evade captivity and take part in the great retreat.

In April 1918 the 2nd Battalion the Royal Irish

Regiment was once more re-formed and I was appointed to command. We were transferred to the Royal Naval (63rd) Division, taking part with them in all their subsequent victorious actions.

A few months before the end of the war I was wounded in the right hand and sent home on fourteen days' leave. This coincided with Cartwright's successful escape and enabled me to be best man at his wedding.

Here we gave a special thought to our mutual friend, the Commandant at Magdeburg, and sent him a wedding photograph—suitably inscribed!